THE DAY IT SNOWED IN APRIL

A MEMOIR

by

DEVIN DEVASQUEZ

Playboy Playmate, Actress, Author and Emmy winning producer, Devin Devasquez, tells all in this intimate memoir.

Compelling and extraordinary, this is the story of a girl who came from a poor and disadvantaged background, but who grew into a young lady in a setting most can only dream of.

Devin, like a butterfly, flitted in and out of the lives of some of the most powerful men on the planet as she became the woman she is today.

Candid and brave, Devasquez shares her journey from Playboy Playmate and *Star Search* winner to ultimately, Emmy Award winning producer, wife and mom.

And her time as the girlfriend of music icon, Prince.

Preface

Prince Rogers Nelson was an artistic genius that many wanted to be around and were curious about. My memories of my time with him are very precious to me. He has been one of the most inspirational and influential men in my life. I felt privileged to spend the time that I did with him during the Purple Rain Tour in 1985 and I have only shared my treasured recollections of him with selected friends throughout the past thirty years.

Prince's career was exploding and mine was just taking off when we met. Why we crossed paths with each other the way we did has always been somewhat of a mystery to me, but all I know is that I'm glad it happened. Writing this memoir is a way of understanding the mystery and coming to terms with it.

I think the way Prince and I met and the span of our relationship has a very spiritual significance. I am a spiritual person and I pay attention to signs and synchronicity - and there are so many signs around Prince and I. My birthday is June 25 and Prince signed his record deal with Warner Brothers on June 25,

1977. The Purple Rain *album was released on my 21ˢᵗ birthday - June 25ᵗʰ 1984. The beautiful song, "Sometimes It Snows In April," was released on April 21, 1985 during my romance with him – he loved playing it on the piano for me. And he died on April 21, 2016 … thirty-one years to the day that it snowed in April.*

Prince wrote songs that reflected how he felt, based on the people around him at the time. He was extremely happy during the Purple Rain Tour - and I was too, it was the most romantic time we shared together. It was when he won multiple awards including the Oscar, he had a number one single, album and movie. I feel blessed to have shared all these amazing moments with him.

A true Prince fan understands that he speaks honestly about himself through his music's lyrics. He was truly married to his music, something he said many times to me. It was the biggest love of his life.

We had common roots in Louisiana - both his parents are from there and I was born there. This carried a special significance for both of us. Especially when Prince entrusted his father to me in the many times I escorted him to events. I always felt honored to be on the arm of his beloved father.

I want to pay tribute to Prince by giving half of the profit proceeds from my memoir to his charity #YesWeCode. I'm hoping my story will inspire others and I can play a small role in continuing Prince's legacy of giving back to the world through his passion for children's education.

I was apprehensive about baring my heart and soul regarding my time with Prince and asked him for a sign whilst writing this book.

I always follow my intuition and exactly a month after his death, I saw a road sign featuring a single white owl. I thought it was odd seeing a street sign of a white owl and had to take a photo of it.

Then on the night of May 21st, 2016, as a full moon hung ripe in the sky, two white owls appeared at my front door making a screeching sound that reminded me of when Prince screamed onstage!

This was not the usual sound an owl would make and it was also very odd to see white owls in Southern California.

These owls came to my front door making these screaming sounds three nights in a row.

It was the first of many signs that Prince wanted me to tell our story now.   I believe he wants people to know him now, through the stories of those who had the privilege to know him "in this thing called life."

And now for the first time I will share with you, the esteemed public, the entire story of my time with Prince.

Acknowledgements

I'd like to thank my wonderful husband Ronn Moss for always encouraging me to follow my instincts. David Chan for his belief in me and for his guidance throughout my life. Laura Russell-Poe for always being there for me. JoNell Gay, I couldn't have done it to begin with without your unconditional love and support. Fiona Horne, you are my soul sister and I truly appreciate how you saw and supported my vision. And finally, thank you for your expert guidance, Casey DeFranco.

This book is dedicated to anyone who has the courage to dream big and believe. Dreams do come true!

Chapters

Chapter 1

"My Name Is Prince"

Long ago and not too far away, in a place called Minneapolis, lived a little Prince who mesmerized all who knew him. Standing only 5'2" with a colorful, flamboyant style that was as unique as he, the little Prince could hypnotize you to fall in love with him. His music left you in awe - it was like he was from another world.

Many called him a musical genius but he could also dance like James Brown doing acrobatic splits in tight pants and high heels! He could sing like no other and made you feel emotions you didn't even know you had, with his high falsettos and sky high sexual energy.

He spoke to you with his sweet eyes, painted with a hint of eyeliner and mascara and his warm, boyish smile. His song lyrics welcomed you into his world as if you were a character in a movie. He had many beautiful women that he called lovers and many he called friends. Yet there was mystery about the little Prince, for many who knew him didn't really know him at all. They were merely privileged enough to be graced by his presence for a period of time. I was no exception; my encounter with the little Prince began by a chance meeting in Chicago two weeks before Christmas in 1984.

The little Prince had a hit movie in the theaters called *Purple Rain*, and many people were comparing me to the leading lady in it, Apollonia. I had my own aspirations at the time as a model for *Playboy* magazine and was shooting photos for my layout as Miss June 1985. I knew something of the little Prince. I did not know he would become a big part of my life and I would be forever changed as a result of our fateful meeting.

While shooting my *Playboy* centerfold layout, photographer Richard Fegley was playing the *Purple Rain* album and like so many others, comparing me to Apollonia. This was at a time when you just didn't see many dark haired, exotic women in the pages of *Playboy* magazine.

It was the mid-80s and times were changing in film and magazines because of the success of the movie, *Flashdance* and Jennifer Beals … whom I also was compared to. The hot look during these times, were the blue-eyed blondes dominating film, television, and print. Apollonia had dark hair, olive skin and dark eyes. So did I. So did Jennifer Beals! But that was about it. Therefore, my chances in showbiz of any kind would place me an underdog. I would think Prince felt somewhat the same way with his looks and his music. However, what dark exotic beauties had was sex appeal and that raw, sexiness was what the little Prince and I shared.

While shooting photos of me in the Chicago Playboy studios, Richard Fegley got the bright idea that he and I would go to see Prince perform in concert, since he was in Chicago for an entire week performing on his *Purple Rain* Tour. I had no objection and had already seen the concert with a couple of friends who were big fans. I thought it was a great concert, but I really wasn't a fan at that time and had not seen the movie of the same name yet. However, that evening Richard and I attended the Purple Rain concert where I saw Prince for the second time. We had decent seats and my view of him was good. Now I was amazed at how he commanded the stage with his dancing and singing and how many times he changed outfits throughout the performance. It was as if you were watching a music video on MTV - (back then MTV played music videos!)

Prince had a way about him, an aura of excitement, unlike anything I had ever seen. He even had a guitar solo at the end of the concert where he was shirtless and would spray the audience with water from his guitar! It was like he was having an orgasm with the audience! (He would later tell me that he did indeed have orgasms during those guitar solos sometimes.)

Seeing the *Purple Rain* concert a second time was even more exciting and made me appreciate his uniqueness even more. He was an incredible performer to do the same energetic show and have it be just as amazing as it was the night before.

After the show, Richard went to the bodyguard that was guarding the backstage entrance and introduced me as an upcoming Playboy Playmate showing his *Playboy* credentials in order to get a photo of me with the little Prince. The big brawny guy curtly turned us away saying Prince didn't like to take photos. We left - Richard was disappointed, but I was not upset.

The next day Richard was continuing our *Playboy* layout and clearly still upset over not getting that photo. Richard Fegley was a handsome man in his late forties or early fifties. His hair was totally white and he was a soft-spoken, very serious, photographer. Richard had shot some of the most memorable Playboy Playmates in the history of that magazine for many years and never had he heard of a rock star not wanting to take photos with a centerfold? He suggested *Playboy*'s publicity department contact Prince's since he was in Chicago for the entire week, to organize a private meeting between us. Prince's team agreed and a date was set.

I was sent off with the secretary of one of the Playboy editors, a young, spunky girl in her early 20s named, Kandi Kline. Kandi was to escort me to meet Prince's publicist at the prestigious Pump Room, which was located at the Ambassador East Hotel in downtown Chicago. Kandi was a Prince fan and knew he was very reclusive and private and that the chances of meeting him were very slim. Still, we were both feeling lucky and had hopes that it would all work out.

However, during the meeting the publicist informed us of what I had already heard from the security bodyguard at the concert the night before, "I'm sorry but Prince does not like to take photos."

It all seemed like a complete waste of time but just as Kandi and I were leaving the hotel, a man in a Purple Rain jacket came running up to me.

"Miss! Excuse me, miss! Are you a model?"

"Yes," I answered.

He glanced at the portfolio of photos I was carrying and asked to see them. He leafed through a few pages before introducing himself as Wally, Prince's bodyguard, and asked if he could show my photos to Prince? I explained who I was and why we were there and he quickly took my portfolio and said he'd be right back as he disappeared up the elevator.

I turned to Kandi feeling a bit vulnerable having my precious portfolio taken away from me by a complete stranger. As a model, those photos were everything to me at that time. I had worked really hard accumulating a variety of images and tear sheets to get work as a new model in Chicago, so I was a bit nervous. "What if he just took my photos Kandi and he's not coming back?"

Just as I said that, Wally appeared. He handed my portfolio back to me and said, "Prince would like to meet you."

Kandi looked excited and I thought we would just go right then and there to get that photo with Prince! However, Wally informed us that Prince wanted us to come to the concert that night. Even though I had already seen the concert the night before, Kandi's eager eyes were pleading with me to of course, say, yes!

I was told that a limo would pick me up and take me there and so I went home to tell David Chan the news.

David Chan was like the dad I never had, since I grew up in and out of foster homes. He was a tiny Chinese guy - about 5'4" tall who was also in his mid-50s. A native Canadian, David Chan was a long-time *Playboy* photographer and the one who discovered me, while I was attending college at LSU when I first appeared in *Playboy* for their "Girls of the SEC" pictorial in October 1981.

David traveled a lot shooting for *Playboy*'s college pictorials and was kind enough to take me under his wing to help me with test shots, which led to my centerfold pictorial. He was also generous enough to let me stay with him while I shot my layout.

When I arrived home at David's high-rise two-bedroom apartment, which overlooked Lake Michigan on the 35th floor, I informed him that I was going to the Prince concert again and it looked like I would meet him this time and get that photo for my layout. David was thrilled for me.

I was dressed in one of my best outfits - a black leather dress, my hair high and blown out (as was fashionable at the time) my make-up carefully applied and flawless, when I hopped into the waiting limo.

We arrived at the Rosemount Horizon venue where Wally the bodyguard met us and escorted Kandi and I to our first-row center seats, which excited me because I had never sat in the first row of a concert in my life! The stage was very close.

The concert opened with the song, "Let's Go Crazy," and tons of carnation flowers dropped down on the audience, as Prince and the Revolution took the stage. The excitement was very high for everyone that night! But it seemed like he was playing the whole concert just for me as he smiled coyly at me, and danced and spun around, licking his hand and shaking his butt.

I appreciated the concert the night before, but this front row intimacy made it a bit hard for me not to blush. And I really blushed when at one point during the concert Prince did a split and completely split open the front of his tight pants! He didn't have underwear on and since he was playing his gestures toward me I could see everything! He looked a bit embarrassed when I put my hand to my mouth in complete shock!

There were several outfit changes during his concert and every time he came back onstage in a new outfit he would playfully make eye contact again with me. Songs like "Do Me Baby" and "Take Me With You" were being sung directly to me! It was getting hard for me not to feel like he was totally communicating that he wanted to have sex with me the way he was singing these songs and looking straight at me!

After the concert, Wally came back and informed Kandi and I that Prince wanted to shower before meeting me. He asked us to accompany the crew back to their hotel. We agreed and were placed in a van with another of Prince's bodyguards, Chick, who was one of the biggest guys I had ever met in my life! A former wrestler, Chick was Prince's main bodyguard and was famous for his appearance in the movie "Purple Rain." That evening he would be driving us.

We had started driving and I remember telling Kandi I was hungry and then suddenly everything was spinning out of control! Chick had swerved to avoid hitting something in the road and lost control of the van! All I could think of was that I was going to die at that moment and never see the thousands of photos I had been shooting all week for *Playboy* because of this quest for a photo with the little Prince! The van crashed into a concrete median and I hit my head against the window. Someone smelled gas and screamed that the van was going to blow-up! I was then quickly being pulled out of the van. It was starting to hail – it was the middle of December in Chicago.

"My leather dress was going to be ruined," I thought with my head aching, my hair plastered wet and make up running down my face. All the drivers, roadies and guests had to hitchhike the rest of the way to the hotel in the freezing cold. There were no taxis and we didn't wait for police – we just thumbed down passing cars.

When we arrived at the hotel I could barely stand up, my knees had started shaking so badly. Wally appeared and profusely apologized for the accident, showing Kandi and I to a hotel room telling us to relax, and that he would inform us when Prince was ready to meet me.

I wanted to call David Chan to tell him what had happened, but Kandi told me to lie down and close my eyes to try and relax because my knees would not stop shaking! I think I felt this way because it was a combination of being hungry, tired and traumatized from the accident.

Just as I started to relax, Kandi shook me to open my eyes and when I did, it wasn't Kandi standing over me, it was Prince! I gazed up thinking I was dreaming at first because I just didn't expect him to be looking down on me laying on a bed!

"Hello, I'm Prince."

He reached out his hand, which was covered in a white lace glove. I sat up quickly as he backed away and leaned against the dresser. He seemed so different than the risqué performer onstage. This was not the same person who had been singing directly to me in such a sexually suggestive way. He could hardly look at me and seemed so shy. His curly hair nearly covered one eye and he was wearing black pants that had white buttons down the side and a white ruffled shirt under a black jacket.

I proceeded to tell him all about the accident, which he said he knew nothing of but he appeared sympathetic. Then suddenly he said with a boyish smile, "I heard you were hungry." And there was a table full of all kinds of food being pushed into the room. I thought it was strange he didn't know about the accident, but he had heard I was hungry? I did remember whispering this to Kandi just before the accident, although I was sure no one else heard it. These thoughts ran quickly through my mind, but I did not verbalize them out loud. We had spent the entire day trying to get a photo, so now was my chance!

As I picked at the food, I informed Prince that my centerfold layout was coming out in a few months and that we wanted a photo with him. To my dismay, he said what we had been hearing already all day long. "I'm sorry; I don't like to take photos." I thought I would just break down and cry in that moment. I was so sure he would at least give us a photo, especially after that horrible car accident!

As my mind scrambled, he asked me, "Where are you from?" I figured he thought I was crazy the way I was going on and on about the accident and my centerfold layout. I casually replied, "Louisiana." His large eyes lit up and he told me that his dad was from Louisiana and asked if I had heard of Cottonport? I nodded that I had. Then in a very soft-spoken tone he said that it was Sheila E's birthday the next day and there was going to be a party if I wanted to attend.

I said, "I'm sorry, but I have to fly to Los Angeles tomorrow to finish my *Playboy* layout and meet Hugh Hefner." He seemed a bit stunned that I would turn down his invitation and shook my hand saying, "It was nice to meet you Devin."

After he left Kandi and I prepared to leave not saying much, we were both exhausted and sharing a little disappointment that we didn't get that photo. As we were walking out the door the hotel room's phone rang. I answered it and it was Wally saying Prince wanted to speak to me alone before I left. Kandi and I remained in the room and soon Wally appeared to escort me to Prince's room on a different floor.

He greeted me like a little kid offering me a chocolate chip cookie at the door. He took my hand and led me into the center of the room seating me on a chair. He was a lot more playful and not as shy now and he sat down at the grand piano in the corner of the room and started playing. I sat there in awe. I can't remember what he played. It just sounded incredible. I was mesmerized.

After I don't know how many minutes, he stopped playing and turned to me and said again how lovely it was to meet me and that he hoped I would have a nice Christmas.

He led me to the door and we shook hands and said goodbye. I was surprised at how small his hands were, but even more that I had been invited up to his room. He was starting to cast his spell on me.

Even though I didn't get the photo Richard Fegley so badly wanted for my layout, I was no longer disappointed, only intrigued after meeting Prince. I had never met anyone quite like him before. What an amazing performer onstage, yet so shy and childlike offstage!

What a crazy week I was having, first to meet Prince and the next day to fly to Los Angeles and meet Hugh Hefner for the first time! It all seemed like a dream.

Chapter 2

"If I Were Your Girlfriend"

My trip to Los Angeles seemed rather anti climatic after meeting the little Prince and enduring that car accident. All I could think of was how strange it all was, and the fact that I never even got that photo! However, my *Playboy* layout and finishing my photos were the most important thing on my mind. I was also so excited to see the Playboy Mansion for the very first time!

While shooting my *Playboy* photos everyone from the makeup artists to the other models and photographers gossiped about Hugh Hefner's lifestyle. I had heard all about his current girlfriend Carrie Leigh and the famous Playboy Mansion grotto where everyone swam naked. Erotic Playboy parties, like the Midsummer Night's Dream, were infamous and talked about in hushed tones among Playboy insiders. Now finally, I was heading up to the Mansion – again in a limo feeling excited and bewildered. I began to think back to how my career started with *Playboy*.

I was only 17 years old in Baton Rouge, Louisiana when I had graduated a year early from high school and started attending college at LSU under a grant and a loan in 1981. *Playboy* was scouting for their college pictorial, "Girls of the SEC," and had taken out a full-page ad with their bunny logo in the college newspaper that they were looking for girls.

I had been working two jobs and taking in my first semester studying business when *Playboy* was scouting for this pictorial. I remembered my English teacher had brought a *Playboy* to class discussing the articles just a few weeks prior. I went to see what all the fuss was about out of curiosity, with another girl from my Biology class.

The photographer, David Chan, was taking Polaroid photos of girls in their bikinis, many of whom were waiting in line for their turn. He had a little long-haired Lhasa dog with him that he called, "Mei Ling" and a pretty assistant named, Sheryl, who was helping the girls with their paperwork when I arrived and stayed standing at the back of the room watching. I felt shy. David came up to me and asked me to put on a swimsuit and I said, "Oh, I'm not trying out." He handed me a swimsuit and said, "Why not?"

I figured, "What the heck?" and went into the bathroom and put on the swimsuit. When I came out I was handed a generic questionnaire about myself - my name, height, weight, measurements and what I was studying. I let David take a few Polaroid photos of me and I left the casting not giving it much more thought.

A couple of months later I got a call from David Chan telling me I was one of five girls they had chosen for their pictorial from LSU and asked if I would pose … topless! I had never had a proper look at a *Playboy* magazine before and asked my older girlfriend, JoNell if she would buy one for me to see? When I looked at the magazine for the first time, I was flabbergasted that they would want me in this magazine. The women were all so gorgeous!

David had stressed to me that I had to make up my mind soon and I asked JoNell what I should do. She was a few years older than me and had become like a big sister, letting me stay with her the summer before I moved into the dorms at LSU. We worked together at the department store, DH Holmes as cashiers in the children's department, and at the State Department of Revenue in the clerical department. She told me *Playboy* was a unique and great opportunity that I shouldn't let pass me by. The money I would receive would pay for a whole semester of college for me, so I decided to do it.

My shoot was at a Plantation outside of New Orleans and only David Chan, his makeup artist, Sheryl and a lighting assistant were present, and oh, of course, Mei Ling! After feeling quite nervous about disrobing, I quickly realized no one cared that I was topless, especially when Sheryl went off to take a nap after doing my makeup.

David kept telling me to "smile with my eyes." It seemed as though we took at least a thousand photos of the same pose that day. I remembered David saying I had "boobs like a Playmate." I curiously asked, "How much money did *Playboy* pay Playmates?" He answered, "$15,000, but you will have to take off all your clothes."

When we were leaving the shoot and heading back to the LSU campus, David asked where would be a good place to have a drink. I explained I couldn't drink because I wasn't eighteen yet. His face dropped and all of a sudden there was obvious concern from the *Playboy* team because they had shot photos of me all day and just assumed I was already eighteen like most college girls in their experience. David said that he needed a guardian's signature for the photos. I told him I had been on my own since I was sixteen and didn't have a guardian. They were clearly distressed and it occurred to me tell him about my 'big sister,' JoNell. David asked me if she would provide a signature.

JoNell agreed to sign for me as a guardian and fortunately it turned out I would turn eighteen in the summer before that October issue came out. I think it was because of me that *Playboy* began having girls show their photo ID before commencing taking any photos. It would take me another two years before I worked up the courage to try out for Playmate.

When the issue came out featuring me I lost my student-working job at the State Department of Revenue because of it. This showed me how hypocritical the Deep South could be. I couldn't believe people could look at the magazine and then pass a judgment on the girls posing in it? That had nothing to do with my job performance and opened my eyes to the fact that I wanted more out of life.

I had been engaged by age nineteen to a slightly older guy who lived with his mother and sister. Mark was a handsome twenty-two year old guy who worked as a mechanic. He was very close with his mother and grandmother and had a younger sister. I would have an instant family marrying him. I really thought Mark was a great guy, although he would constantly compare my cooking to his mother's, which really bugged me! I was still very shy in general unless I felt comfortable around someone and Mark seemed like a cool guy, although he showed signs of being very possessive, which I didn't like at all. Mark would also say how wonderful it was that I was chosen for the college pictorial, but he didn't think I was a Playmate.

I remembered what David Chan had said about my boobs looking like a Playmate's. And in defiance of Mark's pronouncement, one day I worked up courage to call David asking if he remembered me?

"Oh yeah, I remember you!" he replied with his broken Chinese accent. He asked me to send photos of what I looked like then, but I told him I couldn't take nude photos with another photographer, so he suggested I send photos of myself in lingerie. It was enough for David to want me come for test shots in Chicago. When I explained that I had very little money, he offered to front me a plane ticket and let me stay with him because he believed I had what it took to become a Playmate.

I broke off my engagement to Mark and headed to Chicago, with only $50 in my pocket and dreams of a better life. It was scary taking such a chance all by myself, but I was determined to become a Playmate. And I was lucky to have met such an amazing man like David Chan who believed in me. I soon got a job as a waitress and paid David back for the plane ticket. We did some test shots and he introduced me to the *Playboy* editors, who decided I was indeed, Playmate material!

My centerfold was shot by Richard Fegley, in a downtown Chicago studio and despite of me having a horrible flu, was miraculously accepted by the editors and Mr. Hefner. I had been given the month of June 1985 in the magazine and now it was time to shoot the rest of my layout, which would take a week or two.

It had taken a year for the dream of being a Playmate to become a reality - all leading to Richard Fegley shooting my centerfold layout and the quest for a photo with Prince and to this very moment in the backseat of a limo on my way to meet Hef.

During that year, I was also working very hard to gain work as a new model in Chicago and adjust to my new life. My goal originally was to save up enough money to go back to college and get my degree without having to work two jobs, but now my life had started to skyrocket in other directions.

My limo pulled up the long driveway at the Playboy Mansion. As I got out looking at the stone walls it looked smaller than I had imagined, but still very grand. I was greeted by a butler and taken to the Playmate guesthouse, a short walk away through the garden.

The Playmate guesthouse was a large cottage located near the tennis courts. It had several bedrooms with twin beds that two Playmates could share per bedroom. This was where Playmates who were shooting their layouts or visiting from out of town stayed. I was told I could order whatever I wished to eat from anywhere in the Mansion, just by picking up the phone anytime, 24/7.

It took me a minute for this all to sink in. As I prepared to unpack my bags two Playmates appeared at the door. Alana Soares and her sister, Leilani. Alana was part Asian with straight, long, gorgeous hair. She lived in Los Angeles and had been a Playmate a year or so prior, but she and her sister were very social and frequented the Mansion. They welcomed me and invited me to join them at a party that evening at record producer, Richard Perry's house. They told me Richard Perry produced the Pointer Sisters, Barbara Streisand and Wilson Phillips, to name a few. It would be my first Hollywood party. I was excited to accept their invitation. But, before that I needed to go to dinner to the main house and formally meet Mr. Hefner.

As I got dressed for the evening, I was feeling a bit nervous about meeting Hugh Hefner for the first time, given all that I had heard about him. He was the world's ultimate 'playboy!' Alana informed me everyone called him 'Hef' and that he was a super nice man.

I told them how I had met Prince, just the night before and they were both surprised and excited for me. They said if I could keep it together for Prince, then I could certainly manage Hef!

When I arrived in the great hall of the Playboy Mansion, all eyes were on me. Still nervous, I was formally introduced to Hef and photos were taken. Standing there in his famous red and black smoking jacket and silk pajama bottoms, he was relaxed and friendly and I was surprised to see him without a pipe in his hands like I had seen in so many photos.

His eyes were warm as he smiled and said, "Welcome to the Playboy Mansion, Devin."

Alana, Leilani and I ate a delicious meal in the dining room of the Mansion with Hef and his friends. They were all older guys who he had clearly known a long time and they shared a special and relaxed camaraderie.

And then it was time for the girls to whisk me off with them to Richard Perry's house.

Arriving at the party I saw all kinds of celebrities, from Vanna White to the Pointer Sisters - all eating and drinking – socializing like being super famous was the most natural thing in the world!

A man walked over and asked me if I wanted to dance. The man was *Purple Rain* star, Morris Day, of all people!

"Hey, I just met a friend of yours!" I said. He replied, "Oh yeah, who's that?"

I smiled, "Prince."

His smile disappeared and he looked upset and sarcastically replied, "That's your problem," and then walked away!

I was completely surprised - it was obvious they were not friends. And the evening continued to be surreal. I was a little southern girl at a real Hollywood party and meeting so many celebrities that I had only seen on television or in movies. I wondered what it all meant and why it was happening to me? I remember going to the bathroom and someone offering me cocaine like it was candy. I politely turned it down because I had never done drugs of any kind in my life! Sure I was there, but I didn't really fit in with this crowd.

When we girls returned back to the Playboy Mansion, the butler gave me a note saying, "Prince, Purple Rain please call Chick" with a number. I immediately called and spoke to Chick, who said that Prince wanted to phone me. I told Chick that Prince could call me at the Mansion, but Chick said he wanted to know when I would be back in Chicago as Prince preferred to call me there. I said I was spending Christmas in Los Angeles and would be back home in Chicago the day after Christmas.

My life was dreamlike and busy at the Mansion, shooting nearly every day that first week for my Playmate video, as well as, getting to know various people who frequented the Mansion such as actors, Tony Curtis and James Caan.

I was being shown the ropes around the Mansion by Alana and Leilani, who seemed to know everyone and I immediately began to feel at home. The Mansion was nothing like I expected. No one was disrespectful, there weren't orgies happening all over the place, but women were sunbathing nude or topless by the pool during the day. One of the women who walked around naked constantly was Hef's girlfriend, Carrie Leigh.

Other Playmates quickly informed me that Carrie Leigh was bi-sexual and that I should be careful if I were ever invited upstairs. Alana told me a story about the colored robes around the mansion. Apparently, only white robes were in Hef's bedroom, so if a girl was wearing a white robe instead of a colored one, that meant she had partied with Hef and Carrie.

I was far from being a party girl nor had I ever partied with a man and a woman so this was kind of scary to me. I just wanted to stay to myself and get through my shoot. One night after a movie screened at the Mansion, the private secretary of Hef who was a Playmate from the 1950s and his former girlfriend, Joni Mathis, came to me and said, "Hef and Carrie Leigh would like to invite you to join them upstairs, Devin," Leilani was standing next to me and whispered in my ear, "Say no Devin."

I politely said to Joni, "I'm so sorry, but I'm really tired and think I need to just go to bed now."

I was a little worried that they would continue asking me and that I would offend them by not going. Soon after that incident, Carrie Leigh befriended me by asking if I would join her for a workout. She was very sweet during our workout and told me how much I looked like Apollonia and I told her all about my encounter with Prince. She seemed very relaxed and normal. Happily, I never got another invite to go upstairs by Joni again.

Soon afterwards, I met another Playmate, Cynthia Brimhall, who told me that she was a close personal friend of Apollonia, and how much I looked like her. It seemed everyone in Los Angeles was constantly comparing us and I wondered if this was why Prince liked me also?

A couple of years before when I was modeling in New Orleans, I had done some work as an extra in a television movie that starred actress, Cloris Leachman and became friends with her son, George who lived in Los Angeles. Now staying at the Mansion, I contacted him and told him I was to be a Playmate. He had invited me to spend Christmas at his house. Because I didn't have family, I accepted. As the holiday approached I was looking forward to this and also looking forward to going back to Chicago and talking to Prince. My first trip to Los Angeles was turning out to be very memorable and I would have a lot to share with him.

Christmas spent at Cloris Leachman's was rather interesting. Her daughter, Dinah, recited poems and Cloris sat right between George and I as if she was keeping tabs on us! The food was amazing however.

Sadly, Cloris' older son Brian died soon after that Christmas of a drug overdose. I was grateful to have shared Christmas with the family before this tragedy struck and changed their lives forever. As years went on, I always loved Cloris as an actress.

I arrived back in Chicago late at night, unpacked my bags, and as soon as my face hit the pillow I fell asleep, completely exhausted from my first Los Angeles trip.

I was awakened by my phone ringing and looked at the clock- it was 2am! Who would be calling me at 2am? I picked it up and the voice on the other line said, "Hello, may I speak to Devin?" It was a very deep masculine voice. I replied, "This is Devin."

The voice softly said, "This is Prince."

I was in complete shock and said, "Do you know what time it is?"

Prince replied, "I'm sorry, but I'm a bit of a night owl."

We immediately launched into a deep conversation as I told Prince about meeting Morris Day at Richard Perry's party and he confirmed they weren't friends any longer. He didn't elaborate on why they weren't friends anymore and I didn't press the issue. I also told him how tired I was about being compared to Apollonia and he said I didn't really look like her that much. He said I looked more like Vanity, going on to explain that he had dated Vanity, but that he had not dated Apollonia. She was just acting as his love interest for the movie, *Purple Rain*.

As we spoke he asked me things like, "Do you believe in God?" He also asked me things like "What did you eat today?" It was just so odd speaking to him and being asked these kinds of regular questions. He seemed very sweet and normal over the phone and not as shy at all even though we hadn't seen each other for some time. We chatted until I could see the break of dawn through my window and as our conversation came to a close, he asked if he could call me again? Of course, I said yes!

Prince continued calling me at 2am every day for the later part of that week. We always talked until the sun rose. After a few calls I began to wonder and asked, "How do I know this is really you because you seem so different over the phone than when we met in person?" He replied, "Well would you like to see me again?" I admit I was terribly curious by this point and immediately said yes. Prince told me his tour manager, Alan Leeds, would be contacting with flight details for me to attend his concert on New Year's Day 1985 in Dallas, Texas.

The next day Alan Leeds phoned me and said that he had a first-class plane ticket to Dallas waiting for me, and a limo would come to pick me up and take me to the airport. When I arrived in Dallas, I was greeted again by Wally the bodyguard, whom I had initially met in Chicago. Wally also gave me a gift from Prince, his new CD, *Around The World In A Day*, wrapped in a note. The note read, "I hope your trip was cool, this is my new CD, it is kind of strange so perhaps you will dig it, see you soon."

The note was written in purple ink and had a little flower clock drawn on it with his name signed. His handwriting was beautiful and very artistic, just like him. I was then ushered off with Wally backstage to Prince's dressing room. When I walked in, Prince was putting on his makeup. I couldn't help but stare at him in the mirror. He looked at me and said, "I bet you have never seen a man put on makeup before, have you?" I tried to be cool but was of course lying, when I replied, "Oh sure I have."

When he finished, he turned around to look at me, smiling as he stood up to kiss me on the cheek. He looked me up and down, taking in my little red riding hood dress and then beckoned me to come with him to the adjoining wardrobe room. He gave me one of his outfits and said, "Here, put this on."

I did as I was told and was amazed that his outfit actually fit me like a glove. He laughed and said I was the only girl he knew who could wear his pants because Apollonia and Vanity's butts were too big! This made me laugh and feel special, especially when he said I could keep the outfit!

I was then escorted to the sound booth in the middle of the arena where the crowd around me screamed Apollonia! Geez, I just couldn't away from it! I guess they all just assumed I was Apollonia because I was dressed in Prince's clothing. I was sitting next to the sound guy in the middle of the arena and introduced to Prince's manager, Steve Fargnoli, as the *Purple Rain* concert, that I had already seen several times began.

Onstage, Prince said, "This song is dedicated to the girl with the red dress on," as he launched into, "Do Me Baby!" OMG! I knew he was referring to me and couldn't help but blush! After the concert, he took me dancing at a nightclub. I noticed that no one from Prince's Revolution band spoke to me. Only Wally, Chick and Prince's manager, Steve communicated with me. And Prince himself.

But Prince did not introduce me to Sheila E. or anyone from the band, and I saw that Wendy and Lisa seemed to give me the stink eye. They were probably wondering, who the hell I was? After dancing, Prince and I went back to the hotel, where Prince's chef, a woman named Randi, asked what I would like for dinner? It must have been 1am by this time and we were just getting around to dinner! I didn't eat much back then, maybe soup and salad. Prince sat at the grand piano that was in his large hotel suite and played the most beautiful music as I ate my dinner. I was totally in awe and mesmerized by his talent.

I asked curiously, "Why do you write such sexual lyrics?"

He replied, "Why do you pose nude?"

I laughed, impressed at how quick witted he was. But after some brief conversation he said, "It's time for you to go to your room now Devin." We said goodnight and I went to my room which was down the hall from his. As soon as I closed the door the phone rang, it was Prince and we talked again for a while.

The next day I flew back to Chicago and Prince pretty much continued to phone me on a regular daily basis. I can see now that was the courtship phase that Prince liked. Calling a girl on the phone was total, old school cool. One time David Chan answered the phone and didn't understand him and kept asking, "Who is this?" I grabbed the phone mortified! I explained to Prince that David is sometimes hard of hearing and like the dad I never had. He was very protective of me. Prince seemed amused that I had such 'protection' and looking back I must have seemed like such a little girl. First having Kandi chaperone me in our first meeting and now David Chan screening my calls from him? It was so funny that one time, Prince called me collect from a pay phone, but got my friend Laura instead of me because I wasn't home. She said he seemed a bit embarrassed and of course she didn't expect to get a collect call from Prince!

Prince called me after he won Grammys that year and also after he won the Oscar, which I proudly watched him win on television. He told me that after the Grammys, Quincy Jones and Michael Jackson had wanted him to participate in the infamous "We Are The World" charity recording, but that he sent Sheila E instead. He seemed to like calling me and talking on the phone and most of our relationship was built like this for he was still on tour and so extremely busy. I was busy too with photo shoots in Chicago. His voice was so nice and deep and sexy. It was easy to talk to Prince on the phone for hours.

One day he asked me if I would like to come to his New Orleans concert at the Superdome because it would be his largest concert ever. He asked if I would escort his dad to that concert. He also said there would be an after-party and that I was welcome to invite some of my friends given I was from Louisiana. I immediately called my friend, Laura Russell who was a big Prince fan and she brought a girlfriend along from Baton Rouge to New Orleans for the concert and after-party.

The routine was pretty much the same as before, except I was introduced to Prince's dad, Mr. Nelson who seemed so sweet and happy to have my girlfriends and I around to keep him company. Mr. Nelson was very much like Prince in his demeanor. He dressed impeccably well in fitted colorful suits and was very soft spoken. It was obvious Prince was very proud of his dad and wanted to be like him. I could tell from previous phone conversations that Prince's dad was extremely important to him and I was honored that he would have me hang out with him.

Mr. Nelson told me stories of when he was playing music in the jazz trio that he met Prince's mother in. Prince was named after that band called The Prince Rogers Trio. During the after party, band members and various other people joined us for a catered Cajun feast of all my favorite dishes such as gumbo, jambalaya, strawberries and cream, and shrimp Creole.

44

When Prince strutted into the room, he flopped himself belly down on the floor and started watching playbacks of his previous concerts. He seemed completely consumed with his work, but was also totally energized and so charming and respectful to my friends, who were very impressed. Sheila E performed a bit and everyone had a great time eating and drinking, while Prince continued watching his concert playbacks. After the party ended, I was sent to my room where he again phoned me and thanked me for helping him with his dad. He had signed a purple tambourine for my friend Laura's 24th birthday and even told us we could keep the expensive plush bathrobes from our rooms!

By the time I went back home to Chicago, I too was becoming quite impressed with Prince. He was extremely charming, respectful and kind to my friends, so how could I not be? And each time I saw him he gave me yet another one of his outfits from his *Purple Rain* Tour to wear and keep. I had now seen the *Purple Rain* Tour several times and was speaking to Prince almost daily on the phone.

We were getting into spring of 1985 and he asked if I would be interested in coming to his Atlanta and Houston shows on his tour bus. By this time, I felt pretty comfortable around him and felt like we were becoming pretty good friends. This was the only way I could see him because he and I both were so extremely busy, so I said yes. I was flown to Atlanta and went through the same procedure as the previous concerts after being given yet another outfit. This time at dinner I said, "Hey Prince, I'm not going to my room tonight," and proceeded to walk around the table and sat on his lap and kissed him for the first time. He looked at me and replied, "Yeah, I guess you are not going to your room tonight, Devin," and this was the first time I spent the night with him.

We only kissed like high school teenagers, both of us with our clothes on. I think he was a bit shy about getting undressed in front of me and so that night we continued kissing and kissing - falling asleep in each other's arms fully clothed! I began to think I was becoming his girlfriend at this point, at least that's the way it seemed at the time.

He certainly seemed to care about me and I was indeed starting to care for him. Prince continued to call me almost daily as we both shared what was going on in our lives. He would sometimes play new music over the phone for me and tell me what was going on with the band and his dad.

I would talk about my modeling jobs and express how much I missed him and talk about making the time to see each other again. His voice was so soft-spoken and soothing, it was just so easy to talk to Prince over the phone because he seemed much more relaxed. He said my voice was musical and he liked it because it comforted him and helped him sleep. I guess that's why he wrote "Bedtime Story" for me. Many times, we would talk until the break of dawn. This ritual was becoming addictive and I began to fall in love with talking to Prince on the phone.

Chapter 3

"I Wanna Be Your Lover"

Prince and I were very comfortable with each other by the spring of 1985. He was an awesome kisser and for me, this was an essential part of our courtship.

I had been sexually abused as a child by my stepfather Frank, and often felt I couldn't care less about sex. The romance of my relationship with Prince and its slow pace was totally cool for me. I think Prince was smart enough to see this and rather than having to be 'a man' all the time he was often playful and almost child-like with me. Prince had a mean sweet tooth and always had cookies, candy and Doritos around in the purple limo to snack on after the concert. Sometimes he would have a private after party of his own and perform again for selected friends and celebrities. I was always excited to be at a show with him! When I had arrived in Atlanta this time, he gave me a purple Kaleidoscope, which I still have to this day. It seemed everything in his world was colored purple and it just so happened that that was also my favorite color.

Prince was always impeccably dressed no matter what he was wearing, but I never saw him in jeans. Although his frame was small, he wore his three to four-inch ankle boot heels which had an elastic strap that would go around the boot heel from the pants to give the elongated illusion of more height. Standing next to him he was about my height of 5 foot and 6 inches.

He also always smelled so yummy! His smell was very unique because he told me he mixed a combination of scents together. It wasn't masculine or feminine, but a combination of both and hard to describe. I just remembered he always smelled good enough to eat and that I liked it.

Prince was in a great mood the afternoon of the second Atlanta show and said, "Come on Devin let's go to sound check." It's funny but I really didn't know what that was and just hopped in the limo holding his hand and realized that his hands were the same size as mine. When we arrived, I sat in the empty arena while he pranced around on stage. When I say prance, that's what Prince did when he walked into a room - or onto a stage. He had an attitude and swagger about his walk, not intentionally, it was a natural presence about him that stood out and made him seem six feet tall.

He was really happy that day and onstage ran around playing each instrument like a little kid. I was amazed that he could even play the saxophone. He seemed like he was again showing off just for me, and as usual I was completely mesmerized and smitten with how playful and childlike he could be.

After the concert, we did the usual with dinner and dancing. He was drawing on my curiosity in more ways than I knew at that time. I felt sexual and when we went back to his hotel room, we immediately began kissing and making out. This time the clothes started to come off for us both and I was amazed at how toned he was.

Prince's abs were washboard - he was in amazing shape all over. His natural instinct was to seduce me but I felt like for the first time I had switched roles with him. As feminine as I was, I felt like the man and like he was the woman because he was resisting me and still did not take off his pants! And even though I was naked he still would not make love to me and just wanted to kiss. This just made me want him more and thinking back, he probably did this on purpose.

Again, we fell asleep in each other's arms and I felt totally frustrated that he didn't want to make love to me! He said I was too much of a distraction and he need to keep his focus on the music because he still had several more shows to do. However, he asked if I wanted to ride on the tour bus to Houston the next day. I feel looking back on this that Prince enjoyed this long sensual seduction of wooing me with music and mystery. I admit it did intrigue me and by now I had seen the movie "Purple Rain." I had my own curiosity about Prince. So far I saw nothing but amazing talent, charm and intrigue as to who this guy was. Why was I becoming so infatuated? Prince was the epitome of "Cool." How could I not want to be by his side?

On the bus ride to Houston was Jerome Benton who played Morris Day's valet in *Purple Rain*. It seemed like Jerome was one of Prince's best buddies and one of the few people allowed to talk to me. Also on the bus was Prince's private bedroom where I stayed with him. The bus had a small living area with a refrigerator and at the back was the bedroom. The bed had a few candles around it and a TV set and was also rather small. We were able to have more intimate talks on this trip as Prince studied my face and he said, "I'm going to direct you in a movie someday." He seemed like he had plans for me. I answered, "I don't know anything about acting, Prince and I've never even seen a script before." He just smiled and then asked, "Can you sing Devin?"

Before answering that question, I told him he couldn't change my name because I had just done that. My real name was Reneé and I had changed it to Devin when I decided to pose for *Playboy*. I didn't want to be a protégé in his shadow like Apollonia or Vanity and then I said, "No, I can't sing."

He said, "Well maybe we can make you a roadie then." It seemed that he was trying to fit me into his world somewhere and somehow and that he was still trying to figure it out. Again, we fell asleep in each other's arms like little kids and woke up in Houston.

After the Houston concert, I stayed in his hotel room, which was a penthouse suite and this time he got naked with me, but still we did not make love. He said it wasn't the right time and again I was too much of a distraction. He did tell me that he wrote a song for me and played the music from it, which sounded very jazzy. He said he was going to put the lyrics to it soon. I asked him why he didn't want the band to talk to me. He said it was because he wanted me to remain a mystery for them.

That night he had a bad dream and woke up in the middle of the night and was looking at me like he didn't know who I was. I asked him if he was okay and what he was dreaming about that upset him so much. He answered seriously, "Demons."

Prince always slept with his makeup on, which included mascara. One morning I said, "You know I've never seen you without your makeup on." He replied, "And you never will."

When I returned to Chicago, I was just as busy with my own career and had non-stop shoots for companies like Sears, Wards and, of course, *Playboy*. Prince continued to call me regularly and called me from Los Angeles on the night he won the Oscar! He seemed to include me in whatever he was doing even when we weren't together. I began to listen to his previous albums like *Controversy* and *1999*, and was so impressed to see that he totally wrote, arranged and produced all his own music. It was clear to me that I was starting to fall in love with him.

One day he called me and said he had a couple of days break and asked me if I wanted to visit him at home in Minneapolis. Prince explained that Minneapolis had colder weather than Chicago, something that I couldn't even imagine! I could never get use to the winters in Chicago being from the deep south of Louisiana and seemed to always have a cold or the sniffles. If you look at my centerfold you can see I had watery eyes because I had the flu when that photo was shot. Prince said I should come and see Minneapolis in the springtime because it was the state with 10,000 lakes and very pretty at that time of the year. Of course, I said yes.

When I arrived in Minneapolis a man named, Duane Nelson greeted me at the terminal. Duane told me he was Prince's brother. He escorted me outside to an awaiting purple BMW and I was shocked to see Prince behind the wheel! I happened to be wearing a raspberry beret that day and he popped in the song. He then took me to visit the newly constructed Paisley Park, his brand-new studio and showed me a video of "Raspberry Beret," telling me the girl in the cartoon was to my surprise, me! Although I didn't inspire the song because it was recorded before he met me, he added the cartoon character as the video's mystery girl after he met me because he was editing that song during our time together.

While driving around Minneapolis on that gorgeous spring day, I asked him about Duane and he explained that he had eight brothers and sisters, but they were all half brothers and sisters due to his parent's divorce and other marriages. He spoke often about his dad to me, but ironically never spoke about his mom. I was actually surprised to learn that both his parent's roots were from Louisiana because he never told me anything about his mom, but obviously adored his dad.

Prince then told me things about his band the Revolution that I didn't know. He said, "You know Wendy and Lisa are lovers and that Wendy had never been with a man and was a virgin." Which surprised me. He also told me Wendy had an identical twin sister named, Susannah. He then asked me casually what was my favorite kind of car? I explained that although I knew how to drive, I didn't need a car because I used the public transportation in Chicago.

We finally arrived at his house in the suburbs of a place called, Chanhassen. He proudly showed me a long car with what was called, 'Suicide doors' and said it was his father's car. 'Suicide doors' were almost like French doors where the doors opened with the handles next to each other. He was proud that this was his dad's car and Prince obviously loved cars. The outside of the house was painted a dark purple. Inside it was a modest three-bedroom house, where he proudly showed me around. Each bedroom had different colored carpet, one was pink, the other one was white and his bedroom was downstairs in the basement just as he had described over the phone.

Prince then said that he wanted to take me to one of his favorite malt shops, and so we hopped back into the car and drove there. He seemed very happy to have me there visiting and enjoyed driving me around and telling me about Minneapolis. He was very proud of his hometown. When we arrived, no one was in the malt shop, so it seemed we had it all to ourselves. He ordered a milkshake and suddenly a lady came in and approached us. She said, "My son knows all of your records can I please have your autograph for him?" Prince reluctantly signed her napkin as he didn't really like signing autographs, but I think since no one else was in the shop he wanted to be polite.

He then said to me, "Yeah, Devin in a couple of months when your centerfold comes out, some lady is going to come up to you and say, my son knows every line of your body, can I please have your autograph for him?" Prince had a great sense of humor and could always make me laugh.

It was nice to see him so normal and relaxed at home. He always seemed to gravitate to the piano when I was around and played the most beautiful music for me. It was apparent that he was indeed courting me and trying to impress me. He then told me that he put lyrics to my song and that it would be on Sheila E's new upcoming album. The name of the song was called, "Bedtime Story" and part of the lyrics he recited to me were: *"Once upon a time there was a princess, she was so fine, but she was all alone because her Prince had no time, stay with me, tell me a bedtime story."* I think this summed up our relationship. He and I both were so busy with our careers that we barely had time to spend with each other and spoke mostly on the phone. When we were together we talked until he fell asleep in my arms. He would say my voice sounded musical and even though I had a slight southern accent and very high-pitched little girl voice, he liked it.

Our time in Minneapolis showed me a different side to Prince. He showed me photos of him and his dad around his house and seemed so down to earth. This made me feel even more comfortable around him - more than when we were in hotels - and that night we made love for the first time. We were in the basement bedroom that was decorated in white with candles lit around the room. The bedroom was very much like the one depicted in "Purple Rain."

Prince was a very tender and passionate lover and all the foreplay we had built up transformed into a beautiful and sweet lovemaking session. There wasn't much talking except with our eyes and our mouth as we kissed with passion and our bodies finally melted together. He lacked nothing in the bedroom and I think Vanity's "Nasty Girl" song where she says she needs seven inches or more had summed things up with Prince. That man is not necessarily his shoe size in that department that's for sure! It seems throughout the years, men and women wanted to know if he was well endowed in that area. The answer is he was absolutely perfect. It's probably why Prince got so many women! Just because he was short in height didn't mean he wasn't normal or above average in the bedroom. Besides, that is a matter of opinion and desire for the woman I would imagine? I just don't think it's lady like to talk about the exact size of it, I mean I didn't exactly get out a measuring tape, but he was more than satisfying for me in that department.

As tender and loving as he could be – he could also get kind of wild! He would look at me and say, "You're so beautiful, you're so fine, Devin," and then he would pick me up in his arms (he was very strong) and proceed to make love to me utilizing every piece of furniture in the bedroom! From the bed...to the chair... to the counter ... it was like 9 ½ weeks! Yet through all of this I only felt adored by him, never rough handled – and again he was so surprisingly strong for his small stature.

I had to fly to Los Angeles to do more video shooting for *Playboy* and Prince had upcoming concerts in Los Angeles, so he said he would be in touch and I could come to the concerts there. I left Minneapolis with a very high feeling of joy and love and looked forward to Los Angeles.

Chapter 4

"Take Me With You"

I had about a month left before my *Playboy* issue would come out and was getting rather nervous. It seemed more and more people were asking me about Prince by this time. I explained Prince was very private and didn't want me to discuss him. Prince had told me he had a bad experience with the press twisting around his words and just didn't like giving interviews. When I arrived in Los Angeles, I had a message at the Mansion from Prince to call him. When I phoned Prince, he asked me if I wanted a hotel room and from the sound of his voice, he obviously didn't want me staying at the Playboy Mansion.

Prince had a way of asking you a question and just by the indication of his tone of voice; you would be able to tell if he wanted you to say yes or no. He asked me, "Do you want a room?" The tone behind that question said, "You better say yes!" He had the purple limo pick me up and put me in a room at the Le

Mondrian hotel. His limo driver informed me that I could call him anytime to take me anywhere I wanted to go, including shopping.

I felt like a bird in a cage during that time waiting for Prince to call at his whim, but accepted that this was how it had to be if I was going to see him. It was becoming obvious that Prince could be a bit possessive when it came to romance. He probably didn't want other guys at the Mansion hitting on me or for me to stray away from my attention being on him? I sensed that Prince was great at getting a girl to fall for him because he used his personality to make up for his lack of height. It didn't bother me at all that he was shorter than me and I had always been attracted to tall men. Prince carried himself with such confidence and he could be very manly and yet very much in touch with his feminine side.

During my time in the hotel room of course as usual, Prince would phone me and check on me. When he asked me if I would like to visit him at the studio, I said yes.

The studio was called Sunset Sound and there was a basketball court outside. Prince asked me to play HORSE with him. HORSE meant getting baskets to spell out the word HORSE. He was a very, very good basketball player and told me that he loved basketball and wanted to be a professional basketball player when he was young, but he wasn't tall enough.

He also told me again that he was married to his music and that I was too much of a distraction, so my visit to the recording studio was not that long before I was sent back to my hotel room. Over the next days the same pattern repeated. He would call me on the phone to check on me and play his latest musical endeavors that he was working on.

By this time I had Hef's girlfriend, Carrie Leigh asking if I could take her to the Prince concert. Word had gotten out that he was performing for a whole week in Los Angeles and Prince told me he had to ensure the critics give him rave reviews. I could indeed bring friends, but he had no time to really spend with me until after these shows. I later heard the story of how once the audience threw things at him onstage when he opened in Los Angeles for The Rolling Stones. I guess it was extremely important for him to blow everyone away with his performances in the City of Angels.

During these concerts I saw Madonna, who had not toured yet and Elizabeth Taylor at his shows. Prince would playfully coax me to come up on stage at the end of the concert with several others from the audience and dance with him for the finale. Dancing in the finale became something I did several times during the *Purple Rain* Tour. I heard Michael Jackson had attended one of these shows in Los Angeles also and it seemed everyone who was anyone either was there or wanted to somehow get tickets. Grace Jones even chatted with me at the Playboy Mansion telling me how much she loved Prince. Word was getting around about our relationship.

After the concerts, Prince would sometimes want to go have a late-night snack with some of his entourage at an old school deli-restaurant in Hollywood called Canters. He would whisper in my ear what he wanted me to tell the waitress he wanted to order. I said, "Why can't you tell her yourself?" And he would reply, "Because I want you to!" These were little signs of how controlling Prince could be, especially with a girlfriend. He would do it playfully, but I think he did this with girls to see how much he could get away with making you do. I would try and challenge him playfully of course and say, "Now why don't you want to talk to people Prince?" He would reply, "I think it's good to have a bit of a mystery." He suggested I try it and not talk so much. It became a joke because Prince really could talk a lot, especially on the phone! If he liked you and you got his sense of humor, he could talk and joke around quite a bit!

As busy as we both were during this time, it was also apparent that he didn't require much food or sleep. Prince would actually sometimes sleep at the recording studio if he slept at all. He would say to me that he wished he didn't have to stop to eat or sleep. That's how much he loved creating music. He was like a little kid who just wanted to play all day and all night until you made him eat his dinner and go to sleep. It's easy to get swept away into your own creativity when you have great musicians, studios, engineers and everyone on call 24/7 even on holidays. That was what Prince had at his fingertips wherever he went. He had studios, even mobile ones ready to go with the sound engineers that he liked working with on call even on holidays just in case he felt like recording something.

Most people didn't last but a couple years with Prince because he could wear them out. He would sometimes work 24 hours straight and other people had lives, kids, marriages, etcetera! He didn't care. He demanded your time be to his if you were on his payroll. I could clearly see this and heard it from others in later times (like the dancer, Cat Glover, who I was soon to introduce to Prince after she was on *Star Search* with me.)

It's easy to see now that you can tell by looking at the songs sung on previous Prince tours that he was all about sex when he was just starting out. But that was to be expected from a teenage boy genius! During *Purple Rain*, his music was evolving and now he was more about love. He's almost telling the audience his own personal movie with a cast of characters that are in his life. I believe that's why Prince enjoyed doing the concert films that he would go on to do *Sign of The Times* and *Graffiti Bridge*. These films allowed Prince to showcase his talent as not only a musician, but as performer and artist.

Earlier Prince songs like, "Head," "I Feel For You" and "I Want To Be Your Lover" spoke volumes about what was on his mind then - sex! And why should a highly energetic, young, fit man like Prince not have a lot of sex? Besides Prince had now crossed over from an R&B performer to a rock star and a pop star.

You could not contain Prince during 1985, he was everywhere. He was indeed a major star. So why shouldn't a rock star and a Playmate go together? Wasn't that an appropriate image for a rock star? I think Prince had the Madonna/Whore complex and wanted the outward perception of being with a wild woman … but he really wanted a lady. That's why he and Vanity didn't work out. Vanity was the mirror female image of himself. Vanity would later say in the press she left Prince because she needed one man to love her and he needed more.

It became apparent to me that Prince had a hard time being with just one woman, although I didn't discover this until way after our romantic relationship had ended. I believe he was so highly energetic and such a genius that he needed a woman who challenged him physically, emotionally and spiritually. This combination was hard for him to find in just one woman. I believed that Shelia E. stimulated and challenged him physically as a female musician. Susannah challenged him mentally and I challenged him spiritually because I was so sweet and naïve.

Prince told me Susan Moonsie was his first love and his high school sweetheart. He spoke fondly of Susan and said she was the first to break his heart. It was hard for Prince to let Susan go once Vanity entered the picture romantically and I think that's what broke Vanity and Prince up. Can you imagine putting them both together to work in the same band, like he did with Vanity 6? There were bound to be problems!

Eventually, most of the women involved with Prince romantically would leave him because he was so possessive, but they all loved him dearly. Prince wrote "When Doves Cry" for Susan Moonsie after she ultimately left him and got married.

I think Prince looked for traits of himself in the women he was drawn to romantically. That's why most of them were the same type physically. The women Prince was involved with at the time of his tours spoke volumes about where he was in life. During his *1999* and *Controversy* Tours, was when he was involved with Vanity and most of his songs were highly sexual. Now with *Purple Rain,* there was another side of Prince that he was trying to show. I think that's why he played the piano whenever we were alone for me. He knew I was more of a romantic and wanted to woo me with his sweet, softer side.

Our relationship was one of mystery and intrigue for both of us - we had never experienced anyone like each other. I may have looked like Apollonia or even Vanity, but I was a sweet naïve girl who didn't want or need anything from Prince. I truly liked him for the person he was showing me - funny, talented and sexy!

And I was one of the only people in his life not on his payroll.

One time he had his purple motorcycle at a rental home in Los Angeles and took me for a ride down La Cienega Blvd. I was a bit nervous because the bike looked bigger than him and I had never ridden on the back of a motorcycle before. This was also before you were required to wear a helmet. It was quite funny seeing people's faces as they waved to Prince when we stopped at red lights on that motorcycle.

Prince had rented Cher's former home and invited me over one night. It had a roof that opened up completely so you could see the moon and the stars and there was an elevator that Prince was intrigued with - he loved taking rides in it. I spent the night and we took a shower together, but he would not get his hair wet. That night he played my song, "Bedtime Story," on the stereo and told me it would be included on Sheila E's album, *Romance 1600*.

I continued to see Prince during his Los Angeles tour and saw that he was very concerned about how his shows were coming across to the critics. All reviews were glowing and positive like his face when I watched him read all his press.

Prince invited me to see one of his final shows in New York since he got such rave reviews in Los Angeles. I flew to New York and stayed with him at the Helmsley Palace Hotel in a huge suite overlooking the city. It was the biggest hotel suite I had ever seen!

My *Playboy* issue had just been released and I was starting to get busier than ever. In fact, as soon as I arrived in New York, I got a call from *Playboy* saying a huge Hollywood producer, Brian Grazer, wanted to see me for a part the next day. Prince was gracious enough to fly me right back and I could not stay for the concert. I was also surprised that Prince said the words, "Goodbye Devin," as I left because he never said that before. I wondered why he said this at this time, but I had to catch a flight back to Los Angeles and take a meeting with Brian Grazer.

When I arrived at Tri-Star pictures, I waited inside Brian Grazer's huge office for about an hour while he talked on the phone. When he got off the phone, he introduced himself and apologized for keeping me waiting and immediately asked me about Prince! I thought this was rather odd and informed him I was just in New York with Prince and that he was gracious enough to fly me to meet with him. Brian told me a bit about the upcoming project, but said there was no script. I was rather relieved since I had never even seen a script before! It seemed Brian Grazer just wanted to meet me and to be honest it rather pissed me off that I had cut my trip with Prince short for a general meeting with Brian Grazer!

I started to wonder if my *Playboy* centerfold would create more of these kinds of encounters with producers and directors. My whole life was starting to take a turn and I felt like I needed to start preparing for it.

After a few days, I had not heard from Prince, which was odd because he had called me almost daily for months. He had given me a number to reach him, so I decided to call him for once. When he came to the phone he shocked me by saying, "Devin, I can't see you anymore because I live with someone now." I was completely thrown by this statement and simply said, "Okay I understand, goodbye."

When I hung up, I felt totally crushed as I was indeed falling in love with him and thought he was falling in love with me.

Although those words were not spoken by either of us, our relationship was moving along so well and seemed so beautiful. He even wrote a song for me. I just didn't understand this man. He was so different from any other man I had ever dated. Maybe that's what he meant when he said goodbye in New York. That he was ending it.

All I knew was that I was really heartbroken and this was a feeling I had never really experienced before. I was already missing him terribly. I had been swept up in six months of hanging out with Prince, flying all over the country and constant phone conversations. How could he just end it like this? Who was he living with? I seemed to have more questions than answers and no way to really find out. And I had no choice but to accept it.

Looking back, I don't know why I didn't ask for more details on who he was living with. I guess I was too stunned to gather the words and it really didn't matter at that point because he was telling me he couldn't see me anymore and I was trying to process that statement. Plus, our conversations were always so sweet and positive. I didn't feel he would respond well to me asking him a bunch of personal questions, especially over the phone.

Years later I ran into Prince's limo driver who remembered picking me up from the Playboy Mansion. He told me I was the nicest girl Prince had ever dated. He said one girl Prince dated, borrowed a little red corvette of his and never brought it back! The limo driver had to go and track her down over a month later to retrieve it!

I was very busy with personal appearances for my centerfold and I was flying all over the country. Could this be the reason why Prince ended things? I wondered about him constantly and tried to keep up with what he was doing in the press. Apparently, he was now in Europe for the last leg of his tour and getting ready to do another movie called *Under the Cherry Moon*. I only had fond thoughts of our time together and was grateful for that.

Then one day about a month after Prince said he couldn't see me anymore I got a call from him. He told me he was in Nice, France and getting ready to shoot his movie, *Under the Cherry Moon*. He said he wasn't happy with the director, Mary Lambert, who was famous for directing Madonna's "Like A Virgin" video, so he was directing it himself! He told me he missed me and asked me if I would come to France and visit him?

I was completely overjoyed to hear from him and flattered by the invitation, but couldn't help but wonder who he was living with and said, "You said you live with someone?" He replied, "Yes, but I miss you." I sensed there was indeed another woman in the picture although he wouldn't say who she was and I was terribly curious. I was hoping he would say it wasn't so and that maybe he just said that to keep away from me because we both were so busy. However, that wasn't the case. I admired his honesty, but declined the invitation because I knew I could not be one of many girls.

I later discovered he was seeing Sheila E during his time with me and I guess that's why he didn't want me to talk to the band. She was accepting of him being with other women as she has since said in her memoir, "The Beat of My Own Drum."

I was a one- man type of woman and Prince was the biggest rock star at that time. No way was I going to subject myself to that no matter how much I wanted to go to France! As much as I wanted to say yes, I knew it would ultimately not be a good move for me to make. He seemed disappointed and again we said goodbye. I knew this time it would most likely be for good.

Chapter 5
"Baby I'm A Star"

The summer of 1985 seemed to fly by and suddenly it was Fall in Chicago, and the city was stunning with autumn leaves and dramatic skies. I was booking more and more modeling jobs, all kind of similar – fashion, cosmetics, lingerie. Until one day I had a casting for a popular TV talent show called *Star Search*. It seemed every model in town was at this audition for the Spokesmodel competition category.

I had often watched the show with David Chan wishing I could be on it. *Star Search* was the first time you saw ordinary people have a shot at stardom and a $100,000 paycheck. It was a talent competition for singers, dancers, comedians, actors and models. *Star Search* was the first time you saw models speak on television as they introduced commercials and upcoming acts. *Star Search* helped start the careers of Britney Spears, Dennis Miller and Rosie O'Donnell. This show certainly seemed like it could jump start any model's career. Even though I was already a Playboy centerfold, I wanted to be a supermodel at that time. I had conquered so much already against the odds. Being an exotic 5'6" model in a world of 5'9" and above blondes was not easy at that time. I stuck out like a sore thumb! Plus, I was still rather shy and had no experience on television. However, my Elite agent, Marie Anderson believed in me and sent me on this audition.

I waited along with a ton of other girls for about an hour when I saw Cindy Crawford walk in and thought, "Why am I here? I'm so not going to get this." Cindy was very popular in Chicago as a model, but she had not reached supermodel status around the country yet. I felt I didn't stand a chance with her being there just as I heard my name being called into the casting room.

As I entered the room I heard a lady say, "I don't want to see another model, I'm so sick of seeing models!" I coyly said, "Can you please see just one more because I've been waiting over an hour." She apologized saying she was just exhausted and quickly flipped through my portfolio of photos. She then asked me to read on camera, "*Star Search* will be back after this word from our sponsors." I was so nervous and just smiled and quickly read through it, anxious to get out of there. I so thought there was no way I would remotely get chosen.

A day later I was completely surprised to get a call from my agent Marie, saying I was one of two girls they chose from

Chicago for the show! I thought the other model was of course Cindy Crawford and was surprised to learn it was actually another model that I knew named, Karen Marie Polnaszek. Karen was a gorgeous blond who had a lot more modeling experience than me and had been the winner of many beauty pageants. I knew her because a guy I dated a few months after my romance with Prince in Chicago was a friend of her boyfriend, who played football for the Chicago Bears.

Unfortunately, the good news came at the time I was already booked for a *Playboy* shoot in Los Angeles. In the mid-1980s *Playboy* videos were starting to become popular staples with the centerfolds and became a requirement. I had committed to a video called, "The Playmate Playoffs," which was going to be a video of two teams of Playmates battling a series of outdoor games in bikinis such as, "Tug of War" and other outdoor games shot at the Playboy Mansion for cash prizes of $6,000 and a mink coat!

Since I still lived in Chicago, I really could use that mink coat and winning $6,000 for each of the six Playmates on each team wasn't bad. I had just started shooting this Playmate Playoff video when I got a call from my agent in Chicago. Marie informed me that *Star Search* needed me to fly to New York to shoot my modeling videos. These were the videos used during each competition segment and they had to be shot in advance. I went to the Playboy producer of the video to inform him of the *Star Search* news. I thought since *Star Search* was the hottest show at that time, *Playboy* would be excited that I made the cut for the Spokesmodel competition. However, I was informed that I could not leave them in the middle of a job to go do another job and if I did they would not work with me again. This certainly would not benefit my chance at 'Playmate of The Year.' I was completely devastated and had to quickly make a decision. I figured it just wasn't meant to be and told Marie I couldn't be in New York. She told me to send flowers to the producers of *Star Search* so that they would keep me in mind for the next season.

I guess luck was somehow on my side and my team won the 'Playboy Playoffs,' so I went back to Chicago with a mink coat and $6,000 in spite of not being able to compete on *Star Search*. I continued to build my career as a model but at a point wanted a new challenge and I decided to take a chance and model in New York.

New York seemed way too fast paced living there rather than visiting - and it was terribly expensive. I wasn't enjoying living there and I was terribly lonely. Again, luck was on my side. Marie called one day to inform me that someone had dropped from the competition on *Star Search* and that they wanted me to take her place. I guess the flowers worked and even though I couldn't compete at the beginning of that season, I ended up competing in the last three shows.

Karen Polnaszek had won several shows and was already one of the three girls in the semi-finals and there was room for one more, so my chances were good if I could win those last three shows. I had to shoot my videos and since I was already in New York this became easy.

While shooting my *Star Search* modeling videos I was again being compared to Apollonia. The producer, Michele Buitin, told me that she wanted to use Prince's song, "Baby I'm A Star" for one of the videos, but that Prince didn't allow his music on television. I told Michele that I had dated him and I could ask his manager if it would be possible to use the song. I called Steve Fargnoli and asked if he could ask Prince for the use of "Baby I'm A Star" for *Star Search*. A few days later, Steve informed me that Prince said, "Yes!"

Michele later told me that Prince gave her the use of "Baby I'm A Star" for free and that there would have been a $10,000 licensing fee for it. I was very impressed with his chivalry!

Chapter 6

"Kiss"

It was now almost mid-December of 1985 and I couldn't help but think about the previous year at this time was when I first met Prince. I was flown out to Los Angeles by *Star Search* to compete and I remembered being there with Prince and how sweet it was for him to say yes to the use of "Baby I'm A Star." I felt like I would somehow connect with him again. At least he knew I was competing on *Star Search* and I so wanted to do well on the show.

I had never done a TV show before and was terribly nervous. They had me staying at the Hyatt hotel on the Sunset Strip right next to the Comedy Store and I started envisioning how my life would change if I were to win *Star Search*, and make the move to the hub of the entertainment world.

Los Angeles was so different from Chicago and I would have to have a car to get around, something I really didn't want because I so hated driving. Los Angeles was huge compared to

Chicago in that everything was so spread out and having a car was a must, especially for auditions. However, the weather was much more agreeable with me and I thought I could move if I were to win the show.

There were all day rehearsals at a theater on Sunset Blvd and the spokesmodel was required to introduce acts and commercials by reading from a teleprompter, and walking down a runway in an evening gown in front of a panel of three celebrity judges before a live audience. The show would be taped and aired on television at a later date.

During one of the rehearsals, a singer who had been winning several shows caught my eye. His name was Joey Gian. Joey and I became fast friends because he sensed how nervous I seemed and would give me a boost of confidence during the rehearsals. He would tell me how beautiful I looked and that I was doing a great job on the show. He would say he thought I had an excellent chance of winning because I had such a unique look and presence. He gave me confidence.

Joey has become quite a singer today and is recognized as a great talent by many people in the music industry. Back then I was grateful he stuck his neck out for me - he's a good guy.

Once the show began there was complete chaos behind the scenes with wardrobe people literally sewing me into skin-tight evening gowns just before I had to walk out onstage! I guess luck was again on my side because I somehow managed to smile my way through the nervousness. I tied with a spokesmodel named Wendy Edmead, who had won a couple of shows and was very comfortable in front of the camera. In fact, she did a lot of voice over commercials. The audience had to break the tie by voting and picked me as the new champion spokesmodel!

I then went on to compete in another show against a tall blond who seemed very confident and won against her. There was only one last show to win and I would be one of the four semi-finalists who would compete down to the two finalists that would compete for the $100,000. Because I still lived in Chicago, I was flying back and forth to do the shows. Each show took about a week to prepare and tape and because I won the first show, my confidence was getting a bit better, however I was still always so nervous about being judged before a live audience. Doing *Star Search* was one of the hardest things I had ever done.

During one of my visits, I was at the Playboy Mansion having lunch with Alana and Leilani, who seemed to always have a celebrity party to take me to. I was quickly becoming a very popular Playmate because of *Star Search* and meeting other celebrities constantly at nightclubs and parties around Hollywood.

One night we were at a popular nightclub called Tramp and I ran into Prince's manager, Steve Fargnoli. Steve was an Italian businessman in his mid-thirties who wore thick black-rimmed glasses. He was thrilled to see me and he told me how proud Prince was of me and that they were all watching me on the show. He also told me that he was asked to be one of the judges in the finals on *Star Search*. I told Steve he had to tell the producers that he knew me or it wouldn't be fair. I wanted to win on my own - fair and square. Steve informed the show that he should not be a judge and another Hollywood manager, Bob Marcucci took his place.

It made me happy to know Prince was indeed watching the show and they were all rooting for me.

I was busier than ever with my modeling career and managed to win my third show when I competed against a model named Keely Shae Smith. Keely went on to marry James Bond actor, Pierce Bronson. That third win put me in the semi-finals and meant I would be going with the other three semi-finalists to New Orleans for a television convention called, "NAPTE." This was an important convention for television shows to sell their existing shows to bigger networks and get syndication worldwide. Lots of shows would send their actors to NAPTE to promote their shows.

During this convention, there was a party with all the celebrities. It was during this party that I ran into Oprah Winfrey again. I remembered she had called me "Little Butt" because she met me at a charity event in Chicago when I was wearing one of Prince's outfits. Oprah remembered me and said, "Hey Little Butt," while we were dancing on the dance floor. I thought this was so cool as she was becoming really famous with her talk show, which was going national at that time. She was also getting a lot of recognition for an Oscar nomination for her role in, "The Color Purple."

By this time, I was talking a lot with Joey Gian who was in the male vocalist category on *Star Search* and had a mad crush on him. Joey was a tall, handsome Italian guy and he had a sexy raspy voice that made girls melt. Not to mention, he was a really good singer. Joey was becoming quite popular already on *Star Search* and had girls screaming in the live audience. He had a girlfriend during that time, but I could tell he liked me a lot and I told him if he ever broke up with his girlfriend to give me a call. I was dating someone in Chicago, although it wasn't serious and I wasn't in love.

I had fallen in love with Prince and still thought of him from time to time, but I knew he was living with someone - although I still did not know who that woman was.

Prince remained a mystery to me, and a man unlike any other I had been with in my life. I was still a rather naïve southern girl and at age 22 had not had many serious boyfriends. I had been engaged at age 19 and if I had stayed in Baton Rouge, I would have probably been married with a couple of kids by the age of 22 like so many of girls I knew from high school.

I felt like I had been so spoiled already by Prince and had to be with a guy who was charming, funny and talented too. I knew that would be a tall order to fill for me and figured I should focus on my career and not a boyfriend at that time. David Chan kept telling me to date and not get serious with anyone because my Playboy obligations would keep me quite busy for that year. He also told me that I would most likely have to move to Los Angeles. This was something I was drawn to but also a bit afraid of. Los Angeles seemed so big and scary to me at that time. The fact that I would need a car and have to drive on the 405 and 101 freeways did not appeal to me. However, I was making friends and working consistently enough to support myself and get an apartment of my own in Chicago, so I figured if I won the

$100,000 on *Star Search*, I would buy a car and make the move to Los Angeles.

It was the beginning of 1986 and 1985 had been quite a year for this little girl from Baton Rouge. It was time to compete in the semi-finals on *Star Search* and then the finals for the $100,000. I knew if I won and moved my whole life would change. I wouldn't have David Chan to guide me anymore, or screen my calls from the Princes of the world, and I would have to be totally on my own.

Luck was still on my side and I won the semi-final show and ended up in the finals against the only other girl to make the cut from the Chicago cattle call, Karen Polnaszek. She changed her name to Karen Marie Thomas for the show, but I thought it was strange that we were the only two girls chosen from Chicago and now we would be competing in the finals against each other for that $100,000.

We got to meet fashion designer Bob Mackie who was famous for all the amazing gowns Cher wore. He would be dressing us personally for the finals. I wasn't really happy with my gowns because they weighed a ton. The beading was so heavy and one had a bit of a train, so under the hot lights onstage they were not the most comfortable.

87

I couldn't believe how far I had gotten on *Star Search* in such a short period of time and against the odds! Many of my Playmate sisters were gossiping and I was hearing that they didn't think I would win because I had already been a Playmate. Karen was a blue- eyed gorgeous blond whom many favored, because that was most popular look during that time. You just didn't see many girls who looked like me on television. The hair stylists on the show would tease my hair so high to give me more height next to those 5'9" models like Karen.

Like I said, it was a miracle already that I had made it that far in such a short time! That was because out of twenty-two shows filmed in a season, the other three girls had won several shows that got them into the semi-finals - leaving a small window for an underdog like me to sweep in and steal the show. I think because of that window of opportunity I may be one of a few or even the only contestant that never lost on that show. As the end drew near I was really beside myself with nerves thinking how much the odds were against me winning that $100,000 - but how much I did want to win it!

The thing that kept me going was the thought of Prince rooting for me, as well as Joey Gian always cheering me on backstage. Joey was lucky enough with his wins and had made it to the finals as a singer, so I was rooting for him also.

After a few weeks of competing and seeing the same people come back you got to know one another. You could feel the excitement in the air backstage and the disappointment when someone you really wanted to win, lost. And the Spokesmodel category was the last that *Star Search* announced the winner of. I would have to watch all my friends compete as singers, dancers, actors, bands and comedians before they would announce the winner in my category. And in that Bob Mackie dress all night! To say I was nervous was an understatement! I couldn't eat all day and rehearsing under that kind of stress, it was really hard to keep from crying.

Suddenly the big night of the finals was upon us and it was show time! The finals took place in early February 1986, and it was a black-tie event that was taped before a live audience. There were a panel of nine judges instead of three for the finals and the final show would air a few weeks later. The Spokesmodel winner would host a live *Star Search* special at Radio City Music Hall in New York with previous $100,000 comedian winner from the previous year, Sinbad. There was a lot of opportunity was riding on this finale. I was indeed happy to have made it that far on a show of this magnitude and did not think I would win, but was trying to keep positive.

Being positive was getting hard to do, especially when Joey Gian lost in his finale. I felt so sad for him because he wanted to win so badly. The show was moving along so quickly that evening and watching one person walk away with that $100,000 and another person walk away with nothing was starting to get to me. I was fighting fatigue from being too nervous to eat and fighting back tears all night.

Another person that I was rooting for that didn't win the finals was Cat Glover in the dance category. (I would later introduce Cat Glover to Prince and she would go on to work with him on his *Sign of The Times* movie and *Lovesexy* Tour.)

Finally, it was my turn. Standing in that Bob Mackie dress, I felt like I was going to pass out watching my videos played on the monitor and by the time Ed McMahon called out my name as the $100,000 winner in the Spokesmodel category I couldn't help but break down and cry!

I had been trying to hold it together all night for the fear of smearing my makeup and looking model perfect, but I could no longer hold back the tears. I couldn't believe I won! It was official now. I would have to move to Los Angeles and get a car!

I went out and quietly celebrated the win with David, the guy I was dating from Chicago. The episode wouldn't air for a few weeks and I wondered if Prince would be watching?

In the following weeks, even before the airing of the Finals, I had all kinds of agents and acting opportunities being presented to me. It was clear it would be necessary to make the LA move. Joey offered to help me because he had already been doing some acting. I liked that idea especially since he had also broken up with his girlfriend and had asked me out on a date.

Dating someone new and making the move to Los Angeles was huge for me. I managed to find an apartment in Santa Monica sharing it with a nice Persian girl and bought myself a new little red Toyota Celica. Joey lived in Hollywood and most of the auditions I had were there, so I would often go visit him. Joey was also a big Michael Jackson fan and I shared my Prince experience with him. He wasn't intimidated and thought it was cool. Like I said, Joey was a good guy.

Chapter 7

"Let's Go Crazy"

I didn't think of myself as an actress and it wasn't something I was actively pursuing in Los Angeles, but I decided to take some acting classes as I settled myself into the LA, laidback lifestyle and started learning how to drive on those scary freeways! It seemed like I was always being invited to some Hollywood party or nightclub, but I preferred staying home as much as possible. I didn't drink or do drugs and I really didn't care much for socializing. I was still a somewhat shy and reserved southern girl. I couldn't believe the luck I was having and that I had actually won $100,000!

It was the day before my *Star Search* winning episode was to air when I got a call from a familiar voice who wanted to congratulate me on my big win. It was Prince! Somehow he knew I'd won. I figured his manager, Steve had told him and given him my number.

I told Prince I had moved to Los Angeles and he replied, "I thought you weren't going to move to LA?"

I said, "Well the weather is much nicer and I have more opportunities, besides you are always here." I went on to say that I felt like someone was watching over me because I couldn't believe my luck in winning and he replied, "Yeah the Devil."

I couldn't believe he said that and asked, "What did you say?"

He replied in a very low voice, "Are you scared?"

"No, I'm not scared of anything!" I said.

"Good," he replied.

We chatted for a few minutes more before saying goodbye. I was happy to hear from him and felt that we were friends. I was also a bit perplexed by what he said, but figured he just playing with me and wanted to get my reaction to such a comment.

Prince was always talking about God and now he mentions the Devil? Although I not a religious person, I am a very spiritual one. I grew up Catholic, but from an early age was curious about all religion and even though I was only 22 years old at that time, I had already been exposed to religions such as, Baptist, Methodist and Seventh Day Adventists. This left me feeling like I didn't want to be part of any organized religion. I wish that I had asked Prince more specific questions regarding exactly what his religious beliefs were, but I just didn't get that heavy into it with him.

Shortly after the call from Prince, I got another call from his manager Steve Fargnoli, also congratulating me. Steve invited me to dinner at his new restaurant in Santa Monica called The Wave. He said 'my friend', meaning Prince, wanted to see me afterward at the popular nightclub, Tramp. I took my new roommate along for the dinner with Steve where he offered to handle any inquiries that may come along as a result of my *Star Search* win. I thought how cool it was that I had such a big manager like Steve to look after my career. He went on to explain that Prince wanted him to look after me. After dinner, we went to Tramp to meet up with Prince. I was excited and a bit nervous to see him because it had been several months.

Prince soon arrived with a few bodyguards and sat next to Steve and I, as he kissed me on the cheek and smiled. It was like old times all over again when he asked me to dance. Tramp was one of the hottest nightclubs in LA at that time and was located in the Beverly Center Mall. It was one of Prince's favorite hangouts and many celebrities and industry people liked to frequent there. Tramp would be a place Steve Fargnoli would often invite me to meet up with Prince and different friends.

Once at Tramp, Eddie Murphy was sitting next to Prince, chatting with him. I was hanging out with some of my girlfriends at another table when Eddie's bodyguard asked me if Eddie could speak with me. I said, "Of course." Eddie came over and said, "I walked in and everybody was talking about Devin and I said, 'Who's Devin?' And they said, 'That's Devin' and I said I have to meet Devin!"

I couldn't help but laugh and put my hand out and replied, "Well, it's nice to meet you Eddie."

He went on to ask me if I wanted to go to a movie with him. I looked over at Prince and wondered if it was some kind of test?

Although we weren't romantically involved anymore, I wondered if he was still living with someone and if we would ever have another chance. I said to Eddie, "I see that you are friends with Prince and we used to date, so I'm sorry, but I don't think that's cool." He looked upset and said, "Well, I'm not that good of friends with him."

But I still said "No thank you." He walked away pissed off at me.

During 1986, I ran into Eddie Murphy several times with Steve Fargnoli at various events and he always seemed like he didn't like me after that meeting at Tramp. Besides, I was still seeing Joey Gian romantically. I always preferred having a boyfriend and never liked being single for long because I hated having to say no to men who would ask me out. I just got asked out so often during this time that it was easier for me to say, "I'm sorry I have a boyfriend." This was also why I wasn't fond of nightclubs.

At a point Steve Fargnoli had me come to his office so he could introduce me to his team. He had me meet a young aggressive manager named, Marc Gurvitz. Marc had set up meetings with agents for me and was already handling the careers of Bill Maher, Dana Carvey, Jon Lovitz and Dennis Miller. I soon had a wonderful agent named, Vicki Light. Vicki was a tall beautiful blond in her early thirties and her office was above the Beverly Hills restaurant, The Ivy which was a favorite Hollywood hangout for power lunches and dinners.

Sometimes Prince would come into Steve's office when I was there and he would always smile and say hello to me. The secretaries would always be in shock that Prince would talk to me because he never talked to anyone they saw. This made me feel special and I wondered why he was so different with me?

Not long after my *Star Search* winning episode aired, *Playboy* magazine editor, Marilyn Grobowski called me into her Santa Monica office for a meeting. I was nervous because she was considered a scary woman to many of the girls. She was also the editor on some of the most beautiful centerfolds and celebrity layouts. I had always wished my centerfold layout were done with her as my editor - instead of it being done in Chicago. I was never really happy with my *Playboy* layout because I was sick when I shot my centerfold and it seemed Playmates shot in Los Angeles had the best layouts.

When I arrived to meet with Marilyn, she informed me that Hef and *Playboy* were very proud of my $100,000 win on *Star Search* and that they wanted to offer me a celebrity pictorial with a *Playboy* cover and that my name would be featured on the cover.

This was extremely prestigious for a Latina girl in the mid-80s because it had never happened before. Marilyn went on to say she wanted to send me to Mexico for a quick weekend shoot and then shoot my cover. I couldn't believe what I was hearing? Playmate of the Year had not even happened yet and I already had a cover and upcoming pictorial to look forward to! Marilyn added that I would be their November 1986 issue.

I was becoming the "It" girl - my name was associated with Prince, *Playboy* and *Star Search* and many producers and directors were knocking on my door.

During the spring of 1986, I was at Tramp one night and this stereotypical Hollywood producer saw me dancing. I say stereotypical because he was middle aged, heavy set and had a cigar in his hand. He walked up to me and asked if I had an agent? I told him my agent was Vicki Light and he said he was going to put me in his movie and he would call Vicki the next day. I just thought he was hitting on me, but to my surprise he did call Vicki and she informed him that I needed my SAG card and that he should give me a line in his movie.

The SAG card is something every actor needs in order to work in union projects. The SAG card is not easy to get because if an actor doesn't have it, they must have a speaking role in a movie to be eligible to get it. It's a catch 22 and many actors wait for a long time to qualify for it so that they can then start getting union jobs and making more money. I got mine within a couple of months of moving to LA and through the stereotypical producer meeting me at Tramp of all places!

I would find out years later that this movie that I got my SAG card from was also a fateful encounter with my future husband, Ronn Moss. You see I got my SAG card saying hello to Ronn's character, Tony, in the movie. Ronn would go on to become Ridge Forrester on the CBS daytime series, *The Bold and The Beautiful*. The name of the movie was *Hot Child In The City* and ironically, Ronn met his now ex-wife and mother of his children also on this movie. I guess you can say my life was becoming a soap opera in some ways!

My career was moving full steam ahead. I had started acting classes, had a great agent and a manager and was going on auditions for commercials and movies. I worked constantly either on modeling jobs, commercials or movies. And there was always a hot party or event to attend in Hollywood.

I would see Prince from time to time at Tramp or events that Steve Fargnoli would invite me to. By this time, I found out that Prince was living with Wendy's twin sister, Susannah. Well, I guess that's why Wendy and Lisa were always giving me the stink eye during the *Purple Rain* Tour.

One night Steve and I were at Tramp and Prince came in with Susannah and I actually talked to her. She was very sweet and feminine and I respected her relationship with Prince. I was happy Prince introduced me to her. I later found out that Prince and Susannah had broken up around the time Prince and I met and then they got back together around the time he broke it off with me. They were now engaged and I was thrilled for them both. I knew she was a singer and that Prince needed someone that could fit into his world and I was so happy we were friends.

Prince called me in the summer of 1986 and asked me if I would escort his father to the premiere of *Under the Cherry Moon*. I was thrilled I would be one of the few friends invited to fly on the Warner Brothers private jet to Sheridan, Wyoming (of all places!) for the premiere. MTV would be covering the event and there would be an after party with Prince performing. I invited Cynthia Brimhall to join me and looked forward to the event. Prince had a big contest going on MTV to take a local girl from Sheridan as his date to the premiere. I started to have press people phone me and ask questions as to what my relationship was with Prince. I had no idea how these people would even get my phone number because I had a private number. I was always extremely careful about not saying too much to the press because I knew Prince wanted me to stay mysterious.

I couldn't help but think back to when Prince phoned me asking me to come to France when he was filming *Under the Cherry Moon* and what would have happened if I had said yes? Maybe I would have been in the movie? He did say he wanted to direct me. Was this the reason I was now under the umbrella of his management? Is this the reason he wanted me around? Seems I wasn't the only person wondering, especially after I escorted his dad to the premiere.

One day Prince was in a big meeting in Steve's office and I happened to be there. When Steve came out of the office, he said that I was going to be in the next Prince movie. I asked what kind of movie? He didn't know yet. But I would be in it. I had just booked my first movie role, playing an Aztec Virgin in a campy movie called, *House 2* and Bill Maher had a small role also. Marc Gurvitz had me meet with the producers of Johnny Carson's *The Tonight Show*. Since I had a movie role and had won *Star Search*, he thought I would be a great fit to go on the show. I passed the producer's meeting and was scheduled as a guest on the show along with Placido Domingo and Robert Kline. When I arrived backstage, there were a couple dozen red roses waiting for me and I still don't know who sent them? I wondered if it was indeed Prince.

Joey was struggling as an actor and depressed over not winning *Star Search* and over the death of his grandmother who raised him. This weighed on our relationship and he decided to get back together with his ex-girlfriend. I was single again by early 1987. Steve told me that Prince and Susannah had broken off their engagement and that his father was in town visiting. Prince had rented a house on Elm Drive in Beverly Hills. It happened to be the same house the Menendez brothers killed their parents in, but Prince rented it before the Menendez family lived there.

I offered to cook for Mr. Nelson and few friends and invited Cat Glover to join me. Cat had been a dancer on *Star Search* with me and I wanted Prince to meet her because I thought she was such a fantastic dancer. I felt optimistic about rekindling things romantically with Prince now that we both were single. He seemed like he was excited about that possibility too. I felt like we kept tabs on each other through Steve because Steve knew of the men I was dating, and by this time we were all comfortable being around each other.

Prince was teaching me to play pool that night and listening to Luther Vandross. He said, "You know Luther Vandross is gay, Devin." I replied, "Well some people think you're gay Prince." He laughed and strutted around the pool table saying, "Well, we know that's not true!"

It was during this time that he shared one of his favorite songs from his *Parade* album called, "Sometimes It Snows In April," which he played on the piano for me. I loved the song. It was like old times, hanging out, laughing and chatting, as we all headed to another hot nightclub that had just opened in town. I kept telling Steve to make Prince pay attention to Cat and would get up and dance with Cat so Prince could watch. Then finally Prince asked Cat to dance.

Later that night I talked Cat up to Prince and spent the night with him. We kissed like high school kids and made mad, passionate love. He gave me one of his new outfits, like the one on the cover of his *Parade* album and it, of course, fit me like a glove. I really felt great about rekindling our romantic relationship at this point.

The next morning, we were having breakfast and Prince told me he would be going to Tramp that evening and he would see me later in the week.

I was completely shocked that he was basically saying he was going to the club without me! He could tell I wasn't accepting that and I could see that this wasn't going to work with him being this controlling. I questioned why I couldn't go and that I didn't like it and he said, "Devin there is a side to me you can never see, we are not compatible."

I knew in that moment that it was best we keep our friendship instead of me becoming his girlfriend and accepted this as a fact. The side I saw of Prince was the good side of him. I had only seen the respectful, charming and romantic side of him. I had heard of the dark side of him, but I just didn't believe it. It was crazy how he could treat some people and many people would put up with it because they wanted to work with him. I had my own career and never needed or asked him for anything. It was enough for me to be his friend and I think he felt the same way. I knew that Jill Jones, Sheila E. and Susannah had all had romantic relationships with Prince by this time. And they all worked with him.

Prince always had a girlfriend and seemed to collect more along the way. He would usually get involved with the women he was grooming as protégées. I didn't want to become one of those women and needed to remain my own person who would make it in Hollywood on my own merits or not make it at all. I also could not be one of many girls and since he had just broken off an engagement with Susannah, it would be apparent that he would play the field for a while.

My *Playboy* cover came out by the fall of 1986 and I remember Prince wrote one of my favorite songs called, "Adore." I wondered if that was written about me because it sure did describe our relationship. The lyrics, "rapping until the sun came up" described our phone calls. And the lyrics, "In a word you were sex," I took as meaning my Playboy role, as well as the fact that he allowed me to make all the moves on him. He was there for me, protecting me with his managers from the perils of Hollywood. I did feel that he adored me in the way I was always treated by him. And I knew he wrote that song during the time my *Playboy* cover came out in November 1986. In my heart, I feel this song is about me.

My career was moving along just fine and I truly didn't want or need to be a Prince protégé. I only wanted to work with him if the project was a good one and Steve knew this. I knew Prince was trying to include me in his creative projects and find the right fit, because he would also make contact and see me when he was visiting Los Angeles.

Cat was told that Prince wanted her for his *Sign o' the Times* Tour and she was thrilled. She had to go to Minneapolis for rehearsals by the early spring of 1987 and would often call me to tell me how hard he was on them because he was such a perfectionist.

I was getting ready to shoot my second movie, *Can't Buy Me Love* - a Disney high school movie. Cat said the tour would be going to Europe for a few months. Steve informed me that Prince was doing a test run of *Sign o' the Times* and took me to see Cat perform before they headed to Europe. I sat right next to Little Richard at that private concert who wore way more makeup than Prince! It was hard to believe that the end of 1986 had flown by so fast and 1987 was upon us. My life was again at a turning point, as I was getting ready to head to Tucson, Arizona to shoot *Can't Buy Me Love* for a month!

I guess you can say I was adjusting to Hollywood.

Chapter 8

"You Got The Look"

Can't Buy Me Love was a high school comedy starring a 19 year old, Patrick Dempsey who was unknown at that time. It was exciting for me because it would be my first speaking role. Although I was 23 years old and the oldest one in the cast, my billing on the movie was nicely high in the credits.

Paula Abdul was the choreographer for the funny "African Anteater Ritual," dance that Patrick Dempsey's character Ronald was attempting to do to be popular with his high school crowd. I played Gerardo Mejia's girlfriend, Iris and was one of the cool kids, but not a cheerleader. I was the vixen that all the boys liked and all the girls considered a slut.

"The girl who gave more rides than Greyhound," was a famous line that was used to describe my character!

It was originally called, *Boy Rents Girl* when Disney ended up buying it and paying over $50,000 to license the Beatles song, "Can't Buy Me Love" as the title. The movie came out in the summer of 1987 and made over $30 million at the box office, which made it one of the most successful high school comedies of the 1980s.

Filming began in January and there was unexpected snow in Tucson, which had not happened in years. Paula Abdul was only a choreographer at that time and not yet famous for her singing. She told me she remembered watching me on *Star Search* and rooted for me to win. She also asked me about Prince. During the filming, she threw out her back and needed to rest so I offered her my dressing room. We all got along well and it was obvious during the filming that this movie would turn out to be a nice little comedy. My leading man, Gerardo, went on to become a music star as Rico Suave. In fact, most of the cast went on to work consistently in television and film.

When I returned to Los Angeles, Steve Fargnoli invited me to visit Prince on the set of his new music video, "Kiss." Whenever Prince was in town, Steve would ask if I wanted to go hang out with my 'friend.'

When we arrived at the set, Prince kissed me on the cheek and looked happy to see me. He congratulated me on the movie and even gave me a couple of the photos taken of him from that shoot. It was obvious Steve kept Prince informed of what was happening in my career and most likely my love life.

I heard later from Steve that Susannah had left Prince for good and I figured that's why Prince was being so friendly. Later we all met up at a nightclub and went dancing. I remember sitting really close to Prince and chatting when his eyes got huge and a look of horror crossed his face as he watched my hair catch on fire from the candle that was burning on the table. His bodyguard grabbed me and put out the fire but my eyebrow was burned off. Prince would tell that story and call me 'marshmallow head' after that incident.

Coincidentally soon afterwards, I met a guy named Valentino, who was dating Vanity and he knew I had dated Prince. He asked if I wanted to go to a party at Vanity's place because he wanted me to meet her. I admit I was also curious to meet Vanity after being compared to her in looks. Prince even said I looked more like her than Apollonia.

Valentino took me to Vanity's apartment in Century City where I met her sister, Patricia. When Vanity came through the door I thought she was absolutely stunning and could see why Prince was so attracted to her. She was like a female version of Prince to me. They had similar features and I do believe that's why Prince has been most attracted to women whom he can find himself in. That's why most of the women Prince dated looked like they all could be sisters.

Vanity was very cool with me and seemed as curious about me as I was about her. Valentino explained to her that Steve Fargnoli was managing me and told her about my *Star Search* win. I went on to explain that Prince and I were just friends and that he thought I looked like her. She seemed flattered and smiled, but I could see there was sadness in her eyes and I sensed she probably still loved Prince.

Prince was busy preparing for the *Sign o' the Times* European tour that summer and I was busier than ever with commercial shoots and various modeling jobs. Cat would call me from Minneapolis and tell me how hard rehearsals were and how Prince didn't seem like he was in a good mood most of the time. I think it was because he didn't really have a girlfriend at that time and *Sign o' the Times* wasn't doing so well with critics nor on the Billboard charts.

Whenever Prince was in Los Angeles, I was always part of the entourage that was around him. We were friends and our romantic time together was over. I think we both knew it was best to keep our friendship instead of trying to be in a romantic relationship. I saw him at clubs with actress, Troy Beyer and heard about other girls that he was trying to date, but to me, he just didn't seem as happy as he was when we were together.

When he paired up with Sheena Easton for "U Got The Look" and "Kiss" became a hit, Prince seemed a bit happier. Steve invited me to join them for a vacation in Maui that summer. Prince had rented a big house and would 'maybe' join us. We saw waterfalls from a helicopter and drove jeeps around the island, as well as enjoyed the house. Then we all flew back to the mainland and Paisley Park. Cat was excited to be working so much with Prince and Steve wanted me to watch Prince and Cat do some pickup shots for the *Sign o' the Times* concert film. Paisley Park had a soundstage and Prince was directing this footage that was replicated from the actual concerts. I felt Steve was preparing me to somehow work with Prince finally. I wondered if somehow I was going to be included in this one, but *Sign o' the Times* turned into more of a concert film that I had no role in. Besides it seemed as though they were saving me for something bigger acting wise.

As 1987 came to a close, Cat and I enjoyed a Los Angeles Christmas at Steve's Marina Del Rey beach house. I remembered that Steve gave me a bike for Christmas and I knew I wouldn't see Cat, Prince or him for a while because they would be doing the *Lovesexy* Tour in Europe.

My life was taking yet another turn when I went to a modeling event and met Sylvester Stallone. Sly and I began dating at the beginning of 1988. We were often photographed together in the magazines. I remembered Cat calling me and telling me that she had gone to see a Stallone movie with Prince and Sheila E. Sheila told Prince that I was dating Stallone and Prince was very upset about it. This surprised me given that we had not been romantically involved in a long time and were just friends.

My life was so full and good - little did I know that soon I would have to make a very difficult, life changing decision.

Chapter 9

"Sign of The Times"

As I embraced life as a Hollywood actress and living in Los Angeles, two years had flown by in a blink. In 1988 I worked consistently, acting in national commercials for Diet Coke, Budweiser, Miller Beer, Dunkin Donuts and Taco Bell to name a few. I even did a Kirin Beer commercial for Japan with Gene Hackman. And I was getting ready to star in my first leading role as Clarissa Carlyn, in the dark comedy thriller called, "Society." On top of it all, I was dating the hottest action star at the time, Sly Stallone.

Sly was getting over his brief marriage to model Brigitte Nielson at the time I dated him and he seemed like the consummate playboy who was out with a different girl every night, that the press called, "Flavors of the Month." I knew this would probably not last for me, but Sly was a talented artist and a sensitive, funny guy. When Sly called me, his voice was totally recognizable and his office happened to be in Santa Monica where I lived. Sly wanted me to have lunch with him at his office, but I had to decline because I had a missing tooth!

Since I have a big broad smile and this was my eye-tooth, it looked as though Rocky had knocked it out. You see, I had a permanent tooth that had grown sideways under my gums. I was told I would have to have surgery to pull it down and had to wear a retainer at night to put it into place. My career as a model and actress depended on my smile and at that particular time I was waiting for the surgery and didn't expect a call from Sly Stallone asking me out!

I explained my tooth situation to Sly and he thought it was hilarious and wanted to see me even more just to see the missing tooth! This got my relationship with Sly off to a fun start. I actually did agree to have lunch with Sly at his office in Santa Monica, just so he could see my missing tooth!

Unlike Prince, Sly was cool about taking photos and also romantic in that he wrote a poem for me that he gave me on our first dinner date.

When Sly first met me at a Los Angeles Elite modeling event, I was dressed all in white and seemed very mysterious to him.

The poem read:

*"In the silence of darkness when the evening embraces the
city*
A man looks to his soul never wanting to show the pity
*Pity for the emptiness that he sees in the faces of most
who come to pass*
*A vision in white, elegant as the night, entered my senses
so bold*
She stood like a masterpiece
*Painted by artist, desired by many, but too valuable to
ever be sold*
My eyes I did offer a knowing glance
*Her stare was full of mystery and our imaginations did
dance*
*The thought of her stayed as wandered the night,
awaiting the moment*
This Lady in white would once again return to my sight
*The time draws near and this I do know, from the first that
I saw her*
It had to be so."

I was very much impressed with Sly's poem and since my
tooth was now fixed, I looked forward to our first official dinner

date. The plan was to have dinner at the beach, so I thought that meant a restaurant in Malibu on the beach.

Instead, Sly picked me up in his black Porsche and took me to his beach house in Malibu where his chef, Kevin prepared dinner and he talked a lot about his ex-wife Brigitte. I could tell he had a lot of residual anger towards her. However, Sly was very sweet and sensitive, as well as funny, so I was drawn to him quickly.

After dinner, he said he couldn't take me home and had let his staff go for the evening and would take me home in the morning. I had an audition the next morning and I felt very uncomfortable with this situation. He was coming on a bit too strong with me, which I did not like at all and he seemed pissed that I refused his advances. The next morning, I was actually in tears from his attitude and was surprised when he said he would be taking me home himself.

When we arrived at my apartment, he said, "I really like you Devin, so I'm going to give you one more chance, do you want to go back to my office?" I was completely shocked that he was again implying that he wanted me to have sex with him! I turned to him and lost it saying, "You have the wrong girl and I think you are an asshole!" I got out of the car and slammed the door crying.

I didn't care if I ever saw him again after that evening and I didn't expect to. Then about two weeks later I got a call from Sly and he said, "Perhaps I came on a bit too strong Devin and I apologize, can we give it another try?" I agreed and started to see him again and he was a complete gentleman and moved at a much more respectable pace.

Once I was sick with a cold and Sly called and wanted me to have dinner with him and a small group of people in Malibu at his agent, Ron Meyer's home. I explained that I was terribly sick with a cold and he said, "Just take some cold medicine and come, it's a very small group of people." I took something called Comtrex and went to the dinner party. When I arrived, I was given some Grand Marnier to drink and while having dinner I started to feel really ill. Sly showed me where the bathroom was because I thought I was going to throw up and in that moment, I did throw up - right on Sly!

I was completely embarrassed. Mixing the cold medicine with that liquor was not a good idea. Sly was very sweet and helped clean it up and proceeded to take me home. Thank God no one else saw me throw up on Sly! I called and apologized to Ron Meyer the next day as I nursed my cold. Ron was very understanding that I was ill and really should have not been there to begin with. And I was very impressed at how sweet Sly was about the whole situation.

Sly loved to take me for rides on his motorcycle and we would sometimes go to the range and shoot guns. Once we had dinner with Elton John at the famous Nicky Blair restaurant. Elton had just come out as gay and actually said, "Devin is quite beautiful, she can sit on my face anytime." I couldn't believe what I had heard and with his accent wasn't quite sure if that was indeed what I heard!

Then Sly started laughing and said, "Hey maybe you can convert him Dev."

Sly also introduced me to his trainer, George who he wanted me to train with. George had trained Sly for several of his *Rocky* movies and was from Czechoslovakia and his gym was also in Santa Monica. George thought I had the perfect body and loved training me. Sly also taught me how to eat properly so that I could shape my body correctly with diet and exercise. I was always very skinny and blessed with good genes, but I had no idea how important eating habits were at that time. It's not that I had bad eating habits; I grew up in the south where lots of fried foods were a staple for dinners. Sly and George taught me a lot about how to combine the right foods to get the results you wanted for your physique. Sly ate a lot of protein and veggies and didn't drink a lot of alcohol or eat a lot of sweets. This regime was recommended for me as well.

I also met Sly's mother at the nightclub, Helena's, once with Cornelia Guest, a blue-blooded aristocrat woman who was rumored to have dated Sly also. That encounter was reported in the *National Enquirer* saying I spilled a drink on Cornelia, which didn't happen at all. Dating Sly was becoming a bit more difficult for me, especially when the press did things like this, but I really liked his sense of humor and he was a fascinating man who was extremely talented, yet sensitive. He was an excellent artist painting compelling, abstract paintings. I really loved hanging out with him and his adorable twelve year old son, Sage. Sly would later tell me that Sage dated women who looked a lot like me when he was older. I guess I really made an impression on him.

I was really devastated to learn of Sage's untimely death due to atherosclerosis and ensuing heart attack in 2012 at the young age of 36.

One day I got a call from Sly - he was angry. He said, "You fucked Prince!" I asked who told him that and he replied, "Eddie Murphy." I explained that Eddie didn't like me because I refused a date with him and couldn't even believe Eddie would be talking about me to Sly? I was rather surprised at Sly's reaction and didn't know why he was so upset over Prince to be honest? It made me start to pull away from him.

Although I really liked Sly as a person, I increasingly knew we were not compatible as a couple after a few months of dating. Sly loved the way I dressed when he met me as the 'lady in white,' then all of sudden he wanted to change the way I dressed, saying I was no one's "Playmate" and I should wear Chanel suits. He seemed very controlling and possessive as time went on. And I knew there was no way I could be with any guy who was controlling and possessive. If I could, I would have let Prince get away with controlling me. I was way too independent and wasn't about to let any man control me whatsoever.

I had press people calling me so much I had to change my phone number a couple of times. I even had Brigitte Nielsen calling me trying to get Sly's phone number! Ironically, Brigitte's best friend knew me from Baton Rouge! Dating Sly was something I wasn't use to because he was all over the press and always with different girls. I even had girls calling me to tell me he was with them! When I would ask him about other girls he wasn't honest and would fluff things off, which spoke volumes. There were just too many girls throwing themselves at Sly constantly and I began to ask too many questions. It was just so obvious he was a total player. However, I did take Sly up to the Playboy Mansion for his first time during one of the heavyweight fight nights, when Hef would screen boxing matches instead of the more traditional movies at the Playboy Mansion.

Sly and I mutually decided to call it quits and he started dating model, Jennifer Flavin shortly after me and I started dating a Tennessee boy named, Randy. Randy was a tall, extremely good-looking guy who was only 22 years old. After dating Sly who was 42 then, I felt dating someone around my own age would be better for me. It wasn't the first time I actually dated someone a bit younger than me and I was more comfortable with it. I guess I felt more in control with someone around my own age. My career was going well, but I wanted a good boyfriend in my life and finding a good boyfriend in Hollywood was like finding a four-leaf clover. Hollywood guys were just a bit too much for me to deal with and I was never star struck, so it took a lot to impress me and most of them just didn't impress me at all. I had been in Los Angeles for two years and was becoming distrusting of men.

I was now twenty-four years old and always felt that I wanted to be married by the time I was twenty-five. The acting grind was also starting to concern me because I was always being told I wasn't enough of 'this' and too much of 'that.' So far I had played a sacrificial virgin and a high school vixen in two movies.

Hollywood was becoming a bit scary and lonely for me by this time. When I met Randy, he seemed like a breath of fresh air in my life. Randy was working as a bartender who had come to Hollywood to try his luck, but had firm family roots planted in Knoxville, Tennessee. I could tell he was a down to earth southern boy and we related well.

Randy had soap star good looks and often people would stop and think he was someone that they knew from television. He had both a mom and dad, and step-parents that all got along with each other. He even had grandmothers from both his mother and father that were still alive. He also had an older brother and younger twin sisters. Randy had the family I always dreamed of and he was a polite, respectful guy. I had to have a man who was a gentleman and knew how to treat a lady with respect; otherwise they could never win my heart. I was way too spoiled by Prince in that department. And most guys didn't remotely measure up to Prince. He was indeed one of the most charming men I had ever encountered and had set the bar very high.

I met Randy at a summer party in Malibu where he was a guest and we quickly started spending a lot of time together. He immediately wanted to take me home to meet his family in Knoxville, Tennessee. I felt so happy to have a nice normal guy that didn't seem to play games or have the need for lots of women in his life. He seemed happy to just be with me. Randy's down to earth southern charm was already winning my heart.

We had been dating for a couple of months when I got a call from Sly saying he missed me and offered to take me on a trip to Europe. Sly knew I had never been to Europe and I had expressed how much I wanted to go there. Again Europe was being dangled as a carrot and tempting me. However, I was off to such a great start with Randy and wanted to see where it would take us, so I declined Sly's offer.

Instead, I went to visit Knoxville, Tennessee in the fall and fell in love with its beauty. The trees were colored in shades of yellow, red and orange with crisp clean air that said it was really fall. Randy said that Knoxville had four seasons and it would sometimes snow in the winter. I met Randy's entire family on that trip and felt instantly at home.

As our relationship progressed, it became apparent that Randy's family wanted him to move back to Knoxville soon. His grandmother was getting sick and the family wanted him to now come home since Randy been in LA a couple years trying his hand at showbiz. I began to get nervous and felt that he would be leaving soon. We were just beginning our relationship and I didn't want him to leave. Randy lived in Reseda with his roommate,

Marcus and they worked together at a Malibu beach restaurant called Gladstones.

Thanksgiving 1988 had rolled around and as I was cooking a turkey dinner for Randy, I came down with terrible pains on the left side of stomach. The pain kept getting more and more intense that by midnight I decided to go to the emergency room.

Randy took me to the hospital and to my surprise I was admitted due to a ruptured cyst on my left ovary. I was given Demerol for the pain, the severity of which I had never experienced before and had to spend Thanksgiving in the hospital. All I could have for Thanksgiving was turkey broth because they were prepping me for surgery if the internal bleeding didn't stop. This was all very scary for me since I had never been overnight in a hospital before and I had never had surgery before. I was monitored overnight and my blood was drawn every few hours. Luckily, the next morning the bleeding had stopped and I did not have to have surgery and was released the day after Thanksgiving.

It really felt good to have Randy by my side during this crisis. Just the thought of surgery was so scary. And I hadn't had this kind of a man in my life for a while and felt disenchanted with Hollywood. Going home with Randy for Christmas was incredible.

It was wonderful to spend Christmas with a man as family oriented as Randy and have his whole family embrace me the way that they did.

However, I did not expect Randy to propose marriage! As much as I loved him and his family, marriage was not on my mind and I felt like it was a bit too early. We had only been dating a few months.

Randy explained he needed to move back to Knoxville to be there for his grandmother who was getting ill and he didn't want to lose me. I then had to make a tough decision and knew my life again was taking a major turn. I had put on my Playmate data sheet that my goal was to be loved and in love, living a comfortable life and having my own family. It was my greatest dream. I never had aspirations to be a Hollywood actress and although it was nice and I was successful for the past couple years there, it was not my real passion at that time. I felt like I had already achieved great success as a model and against the odds.

Maybe the universe was giving me what I had wished for and it was time to go to another level in life? I felt a bit scared to be alone in Hollywood and not have love. I mean what is success without love? Do I choose love or career at this point in life? That was the question in my head. I told Randy I would marry him the next year and needed time to tie up things with my life in Los Angeles.

Marc Gurvitz had decided to leave Cavallo, Ruffalo and Fargnoli, to work at Brillstein Gray and my agent Vicki Light contracted MS and was battling her illness. I didn't want to search for other agents and managers and figured these were signs that I was making the right decision. I would get my wish and be married by age twenty-five and to a great, down home southern boy, with a terrific family.

As 1989 rolled around, I was at Paramount studios for an audition of a new FOX sitcom called *Married With Children*. As I was leaving the parking lot to go to my car, a man was running up to me saying, "Miss, oh miss, excuse me, miss!"

When I turned around he seemed surprised and said, "Are you Devin?" He explained that Eddie Murphy was watching me from his office window. I laughed and said, "I guess Eddie thought I was a new girl in town huh?" He asked me to come up and say hello to Eddie and I explained that Eddie wouldn't want to see me and didn't like me. But the man insisted I come and say hello.

When I walked into Eddie's office there were a few other guys in the room and Eddie looked totally surprised to see that it was me instead of a new girl he could ask out.

"Eddie I have a bone to pick with you," I said as I walked through the door. "Why would you tell Sly Stallone I fucked Prince, how do you know what I did with Prince? Were you there?"

Everyone in the room started to laugh and Eddie replied, "Naw… I didn't say that to him, I said you dated Prince, is all."

I walked over to him and held out my hand and said, "I'm getting married and moving to Tennessee soon, what do you say we bury the hatchet and be friends?"

Eddie agreed and I asked him for an autographed photo for Randy who was a big fan. My roommate at that time was a friend of a girl who was dating Eddie's brother, Charles. I offered to cook dinner for them at Eddie's house. I guess it's the southern girl in me, I was always offering to cook for people. It was my way of extending southern hospitality and cooking has always been a passion that I was very good at.

Two weeks later I was at Eddie's house cooking, and I met a man named, Keenan Ivory Wayans. My *Married With Children* episode was airing that evening and Eddie told me to ask Keenan to tape it for me. Keenan explained that he was putting a variety sketch comedy show together for FOX called *In Living Color*.

Soon after the episode of *Married With Children* aired, a lot of controversy surrounded my episode because I was the first woman to take my bra off on prime time television. It apparently ticked off a Michigan housewife who said the show was distasteful and shouldn't be on the air at 8pm at night when children could see it. The controversy played on *Entertainment Tonight* and even made the evening news nationwide. It seems FOX was thinking of cancelling the sitcom, but all the talk about my episode helped keep it on the air. Ed O'Neil and the rest of the cast were grateful for my appearance on the show, which ended up lasting on screen for about thirteen years!

I thought it was ironic that my implied nudity on television was a first.

This episode of *Married With Children* sees Al go looking for Peggy's favorite bra at a lingerie store. I played a girl dressed in lingerie and I ask him if he thinks my boyfriend would like what

I'm wearing. I then ask Al if he thinks my boyfriend would like it without the bra.

You see me from behind unclip the bra and take the bra off with my hands covering my boobs as Al faints. When we shot that scene before a live audience, they had me put pasties over my nipples and shot me offstage, so the audience only saw what was on their TV monitors during that sequence. That episode was shown constantly on the news and talked about so much. That was quite the initiation on television for me after doing several films.

Times in Hollywood were changing!

I became friends with Ed O'Neil who was nothing like his character, Al Bundy. Ed was actually a very serious, well-trained actor and I invited him to a party that Vanity happened to attend. It's really incredible how small of a town Hollywood really is and how often you could run into people you knew within the industry. I guess I was now an official celebrity myself and always running into someone I knew or had worked with, wanted to work with, or some mega star that would want to invite me to a party.

Once at the Playboy Mansion, Tom Cruise was there with a friend and his friend came and asked if I would give Tom my number. I laughed and said, "Why can't he ask me himself?" I guess he was shy and just couldn't bring himself to ask for my number and I didn't give it to his friend. Soon after this incident, Tom started dating Mimi Rogers who became his first wife.

Chapter 10

"I Could Never Take The Place Of Your Man"

By the middle of 1989, I was making plans for a fall wedding in Knoxville. I had done some regular modeling for a bridal company in Los Angeles who offered to let me design my wedding dress. I took the back of one of their dresses that I loved and put it together with another high neck bodice to create a tight fitted dress with an open back and a detachable train. I had always dreamed of an outdoor wedding with each bridesmaid wearing a different color dress.

It turned out that Randy's father had a floral shop, so flowers weren't an issue for us and I wanted a small intimate wedding of about 75 people. I had asked David Chan to give me away and started to continue my plans, when I got a strange notice from my bank in Los Angeles. It appeared I had made a withdrawal of $500 on a date I wasn't even in LA. I had to go to the bank to get to the bottom of what I thought was a big error, only to find out my roommate had stolen my debit card and was taking money from my bank account! She was also supposed to be in my wedding!

This was devastating news to discover whilst in the middle of making all my wedding plans. It was also solidifying how hard it was for me to trust anyone in Los Angeles.

I had invested some of my *Star Search* money into buying a house in Northridge with the intention to move in there before Randy proposed. I had to get that house rented before leaving for Knoxville. I was thrilled that the two goals I wanted so badly had happened. I had purchased my first home and I was getting married to a great guy before age twenty-five. In my mind, there wasn't much more this Louisiana girl wanted. I felt that I had achieved a lot more success than I could have ever imagined and I had grown from a naïve girl into a smart young woman who wanted to be practical with the money I had earned.

David Chan was very proud of my decisions and I felt that I was indeed ready to give up Hollywood for love and marriage. Although this was the right decision for me, many friends thought I was crazy to give up all that I had achieved in Hollywood to get married and move to Tennessee. I was starting to audition for some pretty big movies and coincidentally auditioned for the movie, "Tango and Cash" to play Sly's sister. The part went to Teri

Hatcher, but nevertheless, I was at a different level in my career and just beginning to go up for bigger and better roles when I made my decision to quit Hollywood and get married.

I ran into Sly during this time and told him I was getting married and moving to Knoxville. He laughed and said, "What are you going to do in Tennessee? Watch the cows take a shit?" He said he thought I'd be back one day.

Steve Fargnoli had a big falling out during this time with Prince over money and they parted ways. Seems Prince blamed the failure of the *Sign o' the Times* concert movie on Steve. He felt that Steve wasn't supporting him like before. Steve felt Prince was getting more and more difficult to manage and that Prince was too extravagant with money. Sadly, things were falling apart between the two of them in a very bitter way.

Soon after Steve and Prince split, Steve began managing Sinead O'Conner and moved to London. Sinead ironically made "Nothing Compares 2 You" a hit. Prince had originally written that song for Susannah Melvoin and the group called The Family to sing on their debut album in 1986, but it did not garner any success until Sinead covered it.

Steve knew I was getting married and moving to Tennessee and that I didn't need his help any longer. As we said goodbye, I thought of how I would miss those amazing times we shared, like going dancing with Prince and all the delicious dinners at Steve's restaurant.

Marc Gurvitz was now handling the careers of Jennifer Aniston, Dennis Miller, Jon Lovitz and Bill Maher over at Brillstein Gray. I stopped by his new offices to say goodbye and thanked him for all that he did for my career. Marc was thrilled that I was happy and only wanted that for me.

Even though I left the Hollywood loop, I did keep in touch with Prince's father, Mr. Nelson and would call him from time to time to say hello. He had moved into the purple house that I visited Prince at when I went to Minneapolis in what seemed like a lifetime ago. Cat continued to keep in touch with occasional phone calls, but was traveling overseas constantly with Prince and Sheila E. for the *Lovesexy* Tour. Prince had disbanded The Revolution to everyone's surprise by this time and Sheila E. was now his drummer.

Randy and I were at Helena's one night just before I was set to move to Tennessee and Prince was there. I introduced Randy and Prince stood up and shook his hand, which totally surprised me! People would say Prince could be rude and sometimes he would totally ignore people, especially if they were asking for autographs. He had gotten to the point that he didn't want to give out autographs at all. The press he was getting during that time wasn't always very nice regarding him.

I thought Prince was giving me his blessing by shaking Randy's hand and felt he was being respectful as usual regarding my friends. Randy thought Prince was great and was never jealous or intimidated because I spoke so fondly of my time with him.

Coincidently, I did a commercial just before I left LA and ran into *Purple Rain* co-star, Jerome Benton who had gotten married. His wife had something to do with the production of the commercial I was working on at Universal studios. We talked about Prince a little, but it seemed Prince was not one to keep in touch with friends from the past, even ones as close to him as Jerome. No one seemed to know exactly what was up with Prince? I stopped hearing from Cat eventually and lost touch as people do from traveling and making life changes.

I was getting ready to start a new chapter in my life. Was I ready for this big of a commitment? I thought so. Was I nervous about my decision? You bet I was! But hey life is all about making decisions and each decision helps you attain your destiny.

I also coincidentally worked with Morris Day on a film short that I can't remember the name of now, in which I played a pregnant girl who was angry with him. I thought it was so ironic that I worked with Morris and not Prince as an actress. However, acting was never my real passion and I was just happy to have had the experiences I had in such a short period of time in Hollywood.

My wedding was scheduled for September 23, 1989 in Knoxville and it was going to be my rainbow outdoor wedding that I had always dreamed of. I had to make sure the wedding was scheduled on a day that wasn't a UT football game because no one would come to the wedding! Knoxville was a huge college football city devoted to the University of Tennessee's football team. I was already very familiar with this kind of attitude being from Baton Rouge and attending LSU. In the south, it seemed all men watched football. And I wasn't thrilled about having to plan a wedding around football games to be honest, but I knew this was the life I was choosing.

I still had to wrap up some things in Los Angeles before making the big move to Knoxville. One of those things concerned my roommate who had stolen my debit card and consequently stole money from the bank since I had a line of credit on that debit card and no money in the account. The bank had photos of her making this transaction from an ATM and I had the ability to press felony charges against her. She was from Iran and had aspirations to be a model and could also be deported back. The choice was up to me.

I was very hurt and had never had a friend do such a thing to me. I had taken her to hang out with Prince many times at nightclubs and parties. Many people thought we looked like sisters and she wanted to get her nose and boobs done so that she could model. I had even loaned her money to help her get her boobs done and my friend Laura took care of her down in Baton Rouge where she had the procedure because it was less expensive. It was so hurtful to think she would steal from me on top of all that I had done for her.

I decided not to press charges or deport her, but that she would be on a payment plan to pay me back what I had loaned her and the bank. Over a course of about three years she paid back all the money she owed.

I had to also deal with renting out the house I had purchased in Northridge and also needed about $7,000 to pay for my wedding expenses of food, entertainment and invitations. Most of my money was tied up in investments, IRAs and that house, so I had no idea where I was going to get the money to pay for my wedding. Then the strangest thing happened. I went to the empty Northridge house and had a feeling to look in the mailbox. There I found a residual check from Disney for the movie, *Can't Buy Me Love.* It was over $11,000 and after taxes were deducted the amount was just over $7,000! This was just what I needed to pay for my wedding, so I didn't question how this residual check ended up in the mailbox of an empty house I never lived in...! I just cashed it and paid for my wedding. Since it was the bride's family responsibility to pay for the wedding, I felt I had to foot the bill as much as possible, but Randy's family were supplying flowers and the venue.

I believe the Universe, which is 'God' to me, always took care of me throughout my life. I had been on my own since age 16 and worked two jobs while in college at LSU to make ends meet. I lived with roommates and was always a diligent hard worker and I would set goals that I wanted to achieve year after year. I guess I was practicing creative visualization my whole life because I always seemed to get exactly what I needed when I focused on my true desires.

Prince and I shared similarities in this area. He bounced around when his parents divorced and didn't want to live with his mother because he didn't like his step-father. He went to live with his dad, but his dad threw him out after catching him in bed with a girl at the age of twelve because his dad was religious. After this Prince went to live with André Cymone's family in the basement of their house. André Cymone was Prince's childhood friend from high school and was in his first band.

Prince was fiercely independent, as was I. My mother had a nervous breakdown when I was five years old and I was in and out of foster homes as a result. My stepfather Frank was twenty-five years older than my mother with a third-grade education. He was a mechanic and sexually abused me growing up by coming into my room and touching me when I was sleeping from the age of five. He would also make me touch him. Although he never actually had sex with me, he claimed he was teaching me about sex so I wouldn't get pregnant like my mother did with me.

Sometimes when he would drink, Frank would just come and stare at me taking a bath. I felt like I had no privacy at all with him. It was very difficult for me to feel secure at home because we just moved from one shotgun shack to another constantly.

A shotgun shack is a wooden house in which you can see the back door from the front door. It had a living room, bedroom, kitchen and bath and a lot of times I had to share a room with my mom and stepdad. This was part of the reason buying my own home was always a goal for me. As a child, I would daydream constantly of having my own home and a normal family someday.

We moved around a lot when I was growing up because Frank was always getting laid off of jobs and my mother was in and out of mental institutions. As a result, I went to many different schools and was sometimes bullied, especially by girls because I would get too much attention from the boys.

Whenever my mother was in the mental ward, I was put in a foster home with several other kids that I had to share everything with. I think this made me become more introverted and shy because I just didn't feel that I fit in. Frank would later tell me that he had no choice but to put me in a foster home because he had to work and there was no one to care for me as a child. My mother had the mentality of a teenager and Frank was actually her guardian. When I was 12 years old I found out Frank wasn't really my father and that my real father died in a car crash before I was born. My mother never had the mental capacity to give me much information about my real father, so all I know is that he was a foreign exchange student at LSU.

I had the responsibility to cook and clean the house and I would fight with Frank to go to school. Frank had the opinion that if a woman knew how to cook and read and write a little, then that was enough. I wanted an education so that I could get as far away from him as possible. Frank was also very controlling of me and I wasn't allowed to have phone calls or dates when I was a teenager. He would say that boys were nothing but trouble and he didn't want me getting pregnant. I felt embarrassed about my home life and pretty much kept to myself at school.

Like Prince, I was very shy growing up and didn't have many friends because I didn't stay at one school for very long before we moved on.

My mother was more like a child than an adult and slept a lot due to the medications she was taking. She didn't know how to cook much and so I felt more like the mom with her. My goal was to get out of high school and go to college on a grant and loan so that I could get an education and have a better life. I would dream of having my own house and being married to a wonderful man all the time. This was so important to me growing up. I didn't think I would someday become a Playboy centerfold or have a career in Hollywood.

Although I would daydream about what Hollywood stars were like from watching television, becoming a Hollywood actress was never my goal. I just wanted to get away from Frank. I think Frank's control over me as a child is the reason why I could never let a man control me as an adult.

When I won *Star Search*, Frank would call me and ask for money to help with my mom and many times, I would send it. If I didn't send money, he didn't allow me to see my mom. David Chan told me to stop doing this because it enabled him to continue asking. Frank thought I was very wealthy because I was on television. He didn't realize I had to pay taxes on that money and how expensive it was to live in Los Angeles. He had no concept of how to deal with money and as a result never had any.

I didn't tell Randy much about my life growing up and never wanted to discuss Frank because I was embarrassed. I just said I had no family that would be attending the wedding because my mom was ill and I didn't get along with my stepfather. Randy would sometimes press me to talk more about my family life and it always made me uncomfortable. Looking back, I didn't want to deal with that at that time and I had never had therapy for what had happened to me as a child, so I suppressed a lot of my feelings.

My romantic notions about men were also not realistic. I thought Randy was the perfect guy because he had such a great family. I think I bonded more with the families of the men I had in my life. This is why I kept in touch with Prince's father, Mr. Nelson. At this time in my life, I felt like God was giving me what I always wished for in a man and his family, so I had to choose that over my career and that's why I got married when I did.

As my wedding day approached, I was getting really nervous due to a hurricane that was on the horizon. It was best that we move the wedding into a little white chapel, something I didn't really want. Hurricane Hugo was one of the biggest hurricanes ever forecast to hit and so I had no choice. I'm not religious, but I am spiritual and do believe in Jesus Christ. I just didn't want to get married in a church, but ultimately that's what happened. In a lot of ways this set up what my marriage was to become and I knew when I was walking down the aisle with David Chan that maybe I wasn't quite ready. Still, I had a wonderful wedding.

The reception was held at Randy's aunt's house. I had some high school friends attend, as well as JoNell and Laura as bridesmaids. And even though it wasn't my dream wedding, we had a beautiful time. My life was taking a huge turn and I was a bit scared, but soon I settled into a cute little cottage home that my mother-in-law found for us. She was a realtor in Knoxville and helped decorate it as a wedding present. We were sent on a honeymoon to Mexico and returned to start our new lives out in Knoxville.

Randy worked construction for his uncle and I tried to be the perfect housewife. I sent a wedding photo to Mr. Nelson and would call and chat with him from time to time. He told me whenever Prince would visit him that he would look at the framed wedding photo I sent and smile.

The comparisons to Apollonia were inevitable I guess. But this is me wearing one of my favorite outfits that Prince gifted me from his stage wardrobe during the *Purple Rain* Tour.

Photo courtesy of: John Wehlage

Wearing a Prince outfit that he gifted me–

Oprah called me 'Little Butt.'

Photo courtesy of: John Wehlage

Devin DeVasquez, a *Playboy* centerfold and *Star Search* winner, escorted Prince's dad, John Nelson, to the premiere.

People Magazine - 1986

Me and Mr. Nelson – Prince's father at Prince's Superdome
Concert during the *Purple Rain* Tour, 1985

My 31st birthday party with Mick Jagger as one of my guests.

Randy, Me, Pamela Anderson & Scott Baio at the Playboy
Mansion – Midsummer Party 1988

Nick Simmons, Me and Gene Simmons – Playboy Mansion –
Easter 2002

Randy, Me and Hugh Hefner at the Playboy Mansion in 1988

Me, Carmen Electra and Apollonia at the Playboy Mansion, 2002

Me and Hef in 1985

Me and James Caan

Me and Ed O'Neil

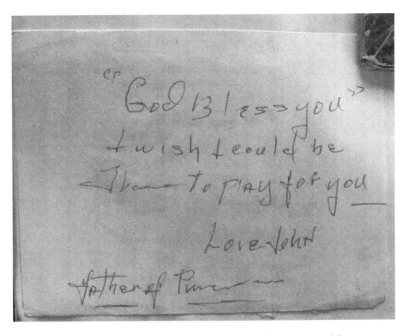

A sweet note from Prince's father to me, for my wedding to Randy.

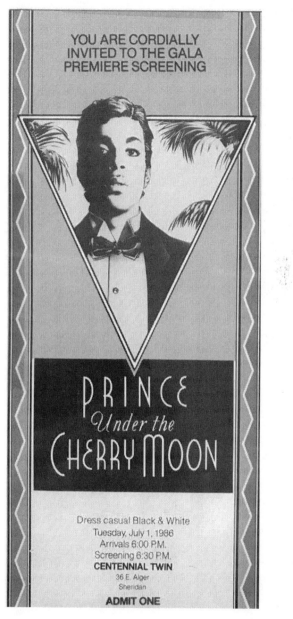

The screening and gala after party for *Under the Cherry Moon* was a night to remember.

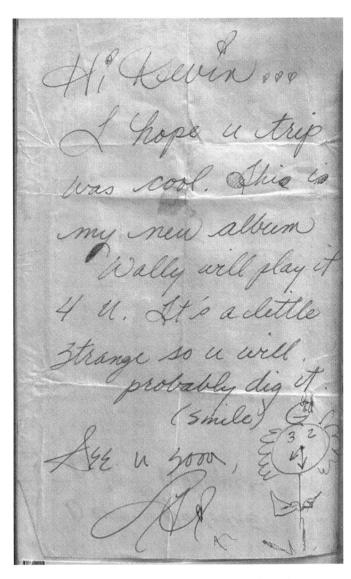

The note that Prince gave me on our first date.

Me and Sly Stallone in his kitchen at his Malibu beach house

Me and Sly in a loving moment

THE '86 GRAND CHAMPIONS

KENNY JAMES
Male Vocalist

JENNY JONES
Comedy

DEVIN DEVASQUEZ
Spokesmodel

SCOTT THOMPSON BAKER
Leading Man

CHRISTOPHER & SNOWY
Dancers

PEGGI BLU
Female Vocalist

TCHUKON
Vocal Group

CYNDI JAMES-REESE
Leading Lady

The 1986 *Star Search* Winners!

Me and Joey Gian in New York City, when I hosted *Star Search* at Radio City Music Hall, 1986

Seth, Hef and Me, New Year's Eve, 1998

Laura Russell, one of my friends who came to meet Prince with me in Louisiana. I am wearing an outfit of his that he gave me.

Dita Von Teese and Me at the Playboy Mansion, 2002

Me and Bill Maher at the Playboy Mansion New Year's Eve 2001

Noel Blanc, Me and Tony Curtis

A modeling photo of me in 1997

The man of my dreams, my soul mate, Ronn Moss

Ronn and Me with his daughters, Creason and Calee on my

perfect wedding day – 25th September, 2009

Me, Ronn, Creason and Calee on a family summer holiday in Cabo, Mexico, 2005

Chapter 11

"Diamonds And Pearls"

I settled into the first year of marriage pretty well. Randy and I would spend a lot of time visiting his grandmothers and his step-parents. I found creativity in editing our wedding footage and putting music to it so that it would be an interesting wedding video. I also started doing some commercials and modeling locally.

I had become friends with Sherrie, a local newscaster who became one of my bridesmaids and she turned me onto many people in Knoxville in their local entertainment industry. Although it wasn't Hollywood, it kept me busy and I would also go to Chicago for modeling jobs from time to time so that I could visit David Chan.

I saw *In Living Color* air and remembered meeting Keenan Ivory Wayans at Eddie Murphy's house when Keenan was just getting that show off the ground. I also tried to keep up with what

Prince was doing, although he rarely made TV appearances and didn't do interviews very much.

I had never had a pet growing up and always wanted a dog. A friend gave me a little Lhasa as a wedding gift and I named her Honey because of her color. My life in the beautiful countryside of Knoxville was now complete with a puppy.

Randy also enjoyed being back home and introduced me to all his old friends. Since he was the most popular guy in his high school, there were many friends that we would run into. We had occasional dinner parties and I practiced my culinary skills daily. I even took up abstract painting. Life in Knoxville moved at a much slower pace than life in Los Angeles to say the least. When I had modeling jobs in Chicago, I got excited.

After the first year of living in Knoxville, Randy shared that he didn't want to work for his family forever and we talked about his goals and desires. He admitted he felt pressed to come back to Knoxville because of his aging grandmothers, but that he wanted more independence from his family. He seemed like he was trying to find what he would be best at and what career would make him happiest.

I suggested that he visit Chicago with me and meet my friend Elliot, who owned several businesses and maybe he could give Randy a job. I thought Randy would be great in whatever he chose to do - he had a very calm demeanor and was great with people. I knew my friend Elliot would see that in him.

We took a trip to Chicago together to see how Randy would like it, having never been to Chicago. We planned to also visit David Chan and I looked forward to showing him around the city. I knew living in Chicago would be hard because I had done that already and never got used to the winters, however I still loved the city and had fond memories from living there.

Elliot did offer Randy a job, managing a chain of car washes that he owned in Phoenix with a partner. He suggested we go visit Phoenix and see if we would like living there. I thought this may be a good idea because Phoenix was just an hour from Los Angeles and I could perhaps get back into my career. Although this was not a priority - my concern was for Randy to feel happy about what he was doing at this point.

Randy and I decided that I we would spend another year in Knoxville and prepare to make the move to Phoenix. He needed time to break the news to his family and we also would need to sell our house and make the move across the country. I felt concerned that his family would blame me for us moving back to the west coast. Randy assured me he would deal with his family.

I then had the opportunity to model in Barcelona, Spain for a couple of months and Randy encouraged me to take it. I had always wanted to visit Europe and declined opportunities from both Prince and Sly to go there. I think Randy knew how much I wanted to go and felt he couldn't afford to take me. I prepared to go there and along the way stop and see London, Paris and Rome, all by myself.

This was a very lonely period in my life. I lived in a tiny model's apartment in Barcelona with other models and had to share one tiny bathroom with four other girls. Every day was spent seeing photographers and hoping to book a job and I missed Randy terribly. I hated the food in Spain because I thought it was too salty and would eat at Burger King constantly.

One day I wandered into a restaurant and met these kids who turned out to be the family of the restaurant owner. They introduced me to Paella, which I loved! It was very similar to Jambalaya. I say they were kids because the son was only 19 years old, but they wanted to show me around Barcelona and I was happy to have friends.

I continued to miss Randy and couldn't wait to get back to Knoxville after only a couple of weeks, but managed to stick it out, staying close to six weeks. On my way back home, I took the train from Spain to Paris with another model and left my purse with my passport on the train! I was stuck at the train station in a complete panic. Luckily, my purse was retrieved and I continued on to Paris. Traveling to these landmark cities alone on a beer budget wasn't what I expected, but it was truly an experience seeing things this way.

Looking back, I can't believe I went there for the first time all by myself. It made me really miss Randy and I couldn't wait to get back home. However, while I was away Randy had some tragic news he didn't want to tell me over the phone. My puppy, Honey had been hit by a car and was killed. I was completely devastated when I was told and felt guilty for not being there to take care of her. When Christmas rolled around Randy got me another Lhasa puppy and I named her, Sugar.

As great as it was to experience Europe for the first time, I was so happy to be back home. I didn't book much work in Spain because I wasn't there very long, but I was glad I went.

Randy and I planned to go to Phoenix and finalize things with his job before telling his family about our plans to move. We had been married for two years by this time and it was now 1991. I seemed to be away a lot and started to realize that I was neglecting Randy intimately. It wasn't intentional and I wasn't interested in anyone else, it's just I didn't desire sex and found myself always trying to get out of having sex. I didn't realize this at the time it was happening, but looking back I had a pattern and was either on my period, away working or had some illness and weeks would go by without us having sex. Randy started to question this and brought it to my attention. I felt guilty and didn't even realize it was becoming an issue.

I rarely felt very sexual it was only something I played for my image. Sex meant I had to be in love because I didn't feel I required it. It was a strange dichotomy because I was a *Playboy* centerfold and many people assumed I must be a sexpot. I think Prince was a lot like me in that he portrayed himself so sexually that you assumed he would be a major player, but in a lot of ways he was somewhat of a prude. Most of the time, Prince had a girlfriend. He wasn't his image and neither was I. We were both workaholics feeding our images, but that wasn't really who we were deep down inside. I started to feel pressure about sex as I did so many times in previous relationships.

In other relationships, I thought the guys were not the right men for me and that when I found the perfect guy there would be no issues with sex. It seemed the men I had been with previously always wanted more sex than I did and now that I had the perfect husband, he was magnifying this issue. Did I have a serious problem? I just didn't care much for sex. Could this be because of what Frank did to me as a child? I was a bit confused myself by it because I just didn't know the answers?

I remembered that my nipples were always erect and I never liked them touched. I couldn't even touch them in the shower because it felt like someone scratching a chalkboard for me. Men assumed because they were erect that I wanted them touched. What did this mean? I didn't know. I would later discover from therapy that I blocked out a lot of emotions from my childhood. I held those emotions in my body and would tense up during sex, which did not allow me to relax and enjoy it and I had never experienced an orgasm as a result. I guess I was raised with the idea that sex was a bad thing, which was why I could only have sex if I thought I was in love. I had never had a one-night stand in my life and always had boyfriends. When I finally talked about Frank touching me as a child, the feeling around my nipples went away and I could actually touch them in the shower without that chalkboard feeling. I had held onto those feelings subconsciously for years.

Frank died a few years before I started therapy, so it was all personal work that I had to do to release those inner feelings. I was never able to confront him.

All I knew during this time was that I needed to pay more attention to my wonderful, amazing husband and I wasn't doing that. I tried to make more of effort to do this. It wasn't a hard task because he was gorgeous and patient with me and I loved him dearly.

One day I got a call from Playmate Cynthia Brimhall telling me about a movie role in an Andy Sidaris film. Andy was a former sports broadcaster with a great sense of humor and his wife, Arlene had been a producer in the *Nancy Drew* and *Hardy Boys* TV series. They were the cutest husband and wife team. Andy directed all their low-budget movies and Arlene produced them. They were the first to garner this niche of action packed films that were shot in beautiful locations with gorgeous women.

These films were known to have Playboy Playmates in them and were usually done in Hawaii. Cynthia had done several of these films and called to tell me about a role that was perfect for me. She said that Andy Sidaris wanted me for the part and I would play opposite Erik Estrada who was already well recognized from his famous role on the TV series, *CHIPS*.

I spoke to Randy about this and he encouraged me to do it even though there would be a love scene with Erik and some nudity. The film would be shot in Lake Havasu and Las Vegas. Randy said he would take the time to settle things with his family and prepare to make the move to Phoenix.

I went on location to Las Vegas to shoot, *Guns* and played opposite Erik Estrada as the drug dealer's girlfriend named Cash. I was a badass girl who killed people! It was fun to be back in front of the camera on a film and I realized that I had missed it. Randy thought it was good for me to get back into acting in Los Angeles while he prepared to make our move to Phoenix.

I was offered a place to stay in Los Angeles with Randy's best friend and old roommate, Marcus. I started getting back into acting classes and auditioned for the *Groundlings* where I made the cut and studied with Lisa Kudrow before she became famous for her role as Phoebe on the TV series, *Friends*. I also made the rounds for commercial auditions and found it harder to break back into things after being gone for a couple of years.

Just as expected, Randy's family blamed me for the decision of wanting to move to Phoenix. I felt sad that they would feel that way and was doing the best I could to stay busy with acting classes and trying to get work in commercials.

Marcus had a young roommate, Casper who had moved in with him from Florida who wanted to become an actor. This guy was always flirting with me and trying to cheer me up if he saw me crying, which I did a lot during this time. I missed Randy and was feeling guilty for neglecting him and I felt sad that his family was blaming me for our move. Marcus warned this guy to keep his distance and Marcus was a big brawny guy that you didn't want to mess with who felt protective of me being his best friend's wife.

During this time, I would occasionally fly back and forth to Knoxville as we finally sold our house and were preparing to move across the country. The plan would be for Randy to pack things up and drive out to get me from Marcus' and we would continue on to Phoenix. I was getting excited about the move. Randy and I had found a house we wanted to buy in Phoenix already. I had booked a couple of commercials and it looked like I was getting my career going again in Los Angeles. We planned that I would just fly back and forth for jobs once we got settled in Phoenix.

Just before Randy was to come for me, I went out to celebrate with Marcus and his roommate and the three of us got a bit drunk that night from too many shots of Jack Daniels. When we arrived back at the apartment, Marcus could hear the gay neighbors having sex next door and started beating on the walls screaming at them. He then broke down with tears in his eyes and told us that he molested by a neighbor when he was a child. Marcus was a bit drunk that night and when he went off to bed I stayed up talking to his roommate.

Shocked to hear this news brought up something in me and I began to cry and told Marcus' roommate that I had also been molested and was surprised that I even told him that. I hadn't even shared that with my husband. I couldn't believe I was telling him all of this and in that moment, he kissed me and started expressing how he hated to see me cry.

He then shared with me that his mother was molested. These secrets seemed to bond us in a strange way and we ended up having sex. I was mortified that I could do such a thing. I had never cheated on a boyfriend so the thought of breaking my marriage vows really made me feel guilty. How could this happen? I wasn't in love with this guy and didn't even know him that well. What really confused me was that I had my very first orgasm. I was 27 years old by now and had never experienced one. I always faked them to get sex over and done with in the past with every lover, even Prince!

All of a sudden, my world was falling apart and I was becoming more and more confused. We did not want Marcus to find out what had happened and I made it clear how much I loved my husband and that this would not happen again. Randy was getting ready to come for me, and this guy wanted to make himself scarce and not even be around when Randy got there. He did ask me to autograph a *Playboy* for him as a keepsake and so I did. I figured this was just a big mistake that I would soon forget and needed to focus on moving now to Phoenix.

When Randy finally arrived, we were alone in the apartment because Marcus was working. The plan was to have dinner with Marcus before leaving. Randy and I were scheduled to leave early one morning within the next couple of days for our drive to Phoenix. To my surprise, Randy woke me up the next morning with the *Playboy* I had signed for Marcus' roommate in his hands and tears in his eyes. I couldn't believe what was happening; it seemed like a bad dream. Randy said he had a feeling and went rummaging around the roommate's room and found the *Playboy*. He had a sixth sense about things and I confessed and told him everything that had happened and he said I needed to get into therapy once we settled in Phoenix. I agreed and we would continue on with our move after our dinner with

Marcus. We also decided we didn't want Marcus to know because we didn't want him to blame himself.

Eventually Marcus' roommate came back home not knowing what had transpired. Randy locked eyes with him in front of Marcus without letting on anything, but I felt so incredibly guilty and depressed.

Once we got to Phoenix, I threw myself into unpacking and finding a good therapist. It was obvious something was wrong with me and I wanted to figure it out. Due to what happened, sex wasn't even on Randy's radar during this time, but he did not want to end our marriage over it and I knew I still loved him. We were going to try and work this out.

I got a call from *Playboy* while unpacking and dealing with all of this emotional drama and they said Prince called and wanted me for his "Diamond and Pearls" video. I would have to be in Los Angeles the next day and I was in no shape for this, so I had no choice but to decline it. Between unpacking and trying to find a therapist there was just no way I could drop everything and catch a flight to LA for a video, even though it was Prince. I often wondered what would have happened if I did do that now? But sometimes we have to make decisions in a moment's notice and I decided the timing was just not right.

Chapter 12

"Call My Name"

My priority was to get a therapist and work on my marriage as I settled into my new life in Phoenix. I was really depressed over what I did to Randy so I focused on getting the new house in order. I unpacked during the day while Randy started his new job as the manager of a chain of car washes. I also found a therapist and it seemed she immediately wanted to put me on antidepressants. I didn't want to take any type of drug, so I didn't want to see her again. I also had a really hard time paying money to a stranger to talk about my deepest darkest secrets. Alone, I just tried to deal with my depression as best as I could.

I began to hate Marcus' roommate for screwing up my life! I hated myself for letting it happen. I just would beat myself up daily during this time and I became extremely depressed. It was starting to becoming harder and harder for me to function around Randy. As much as I loved him, I could not be intimate with him and I could not forgive myself. He came home one day from work and looked at me and said, "You're leaving, aren't you?" I nodded my head and packed only my clothes leaving everything with him, including my dog. I just needed to be by myself to figure things out.

I rented an apartment with Playmate Cynthia Brimhall in Beverly Hills and threw myself into work. Randy did the same thing in Phoenix and we thought maybe after some distance I would come back. But, the more distance we had between us the more apparent it was that my marriage would not survive. It would take me four years to finally file for divorce. I realized I wanted to be in Los Angeles and he realized he wanted to remain in Phoenix.

During this time, Prince had everyone buzzing about him for writing "Slave" on his face. It seemed that Prince had issues of his own by the early '90s. He was in a bitter battle with Warner Brothers over his master recording tapes and did not own his own music. The contract he signed at such a young age gave Warner Brothers all the rights to his major hits like, "Purple Rain." He was still obligated to create a couple more albums, but the problem with Warner Brothers and Prince began to escalate. It seemed Prince wanted to put out his music whenever he wanted it out and Warner Brothers wanted him to wait and not release new stuff so fast. Prince would produce music every single day, so he would often get bored of what he'd just done and want to release new tracks.

His follow up movie to *Purple Rain* was *Graffiti Bridge* which was a huge disappointment for many fans. I wondered if this was the movie I was supposed to have done with him. Critics were really rough on him during this time and hip-hop music was starting to become quite popular. Many critics thought Prince was basically over until he did the soundtrack for the movie, *Batman*.

I had lost touch with his father from moving and going through my own drama in life. And I started to terribly miss those days with Steve and Prince, which now seemed like so long ago in the past. One day I was with a girlfriend who was talking about visiting a friend of hers who was working on a Prince video at Union station in downtown Los Angeles and realized this was the video shoot I was supposed to have done with him! I asked her if I could come along with her to visit her friend on the set.

When we arrived on the set, her friend told us that no one could talk to Prince or even look him in the eyes. He had these girls around him that were in "Diamonds and Pearls" and they were called "The Twins." I knew that would have been my role had I said yes to the video. One of the girls even looked a lot like me. These girls were now in a series of music videos with

Prince. I wished I could have somehow done that video now, but the timing in my life sucked.

Upon hearing from the crew member how no one could talk to Prince, I said, "Watch this." I went right up to Prince and tapped him on his shoulder and as he turned around, I smiled and said, "Hi." He smiled, kissed me on the cheek and said "Hi" back. I asked him about his father and explained that I was moving when he called about me doing the video. We chatted very briefly because he was working and ran off to his dressing room to change clothes. Everyone wondered who I was and how I could just walk up to Prince and talk to him like that!

About a year later on an audition for *Baywatch*, I ran into Carmen Electra whom I had read was a Prince protégé and struck up a conversation with her at the audition. I told her about my dating Prince and asked how he was doing. She told me she wasn't dating him and that he was now with a girl named, Mayte.

Not too long after that meeting, I was doing a play in Hollywood called, *Southern Rapture* with Dwight Yoakum and Vanessa Marcil who was newly on the daytime soap, *General Hospital*. Dwight was friends with Cynthia Brimhall and wanted me for the play because he thought I looked like Vanessa. It was directed by Peter Fonda and would be good for my career. I would do part of the run and Vanessa was to do part of the run. We would share the same role, but perform them at different times.

During the rehearsals, I learned that Vanessa was seeing Prince and told her about my time with him. I knew she was married to Corey Feldman and I had been a friend of Corey's since he was sixteen years old. She claimed she wasn't married to Corey anymore and she was visiting Prince in Minneapolis. I often ran into Vanessa on commercial auditions during that time and she kept mentioning Prince and how she had just come from visiting him in Minneapolis. I asked her if she said hello for me, but she told me she didn't. I began to wonder about Prince because Carmen had just told me he was seeing someone named Mayte. As usual, there were always more questions than answers when it came to Prince.

During the run of this play, my mother died of breast cancer and I had to go back to Baton Rouge, so my performances were cut short. Frank had died of lung cancer a year before my mom.

I was now 30 years old.

I was still in a lot of pain over my failed marriage, my mother's death and trying to get my career back on track. Also during this time, I found new agents and managers and went on a film audition for a movie called *A Low Down Dirty Shame*. My managers said that they were told that the director was writing a part especially for me. The director turned out to be Keenan Ivory Wayans. Again, I was playing the drug dealer's girlfriend, but this was a cast that included Jada Pinkett, and it had a ten million dollar budget. This film debuted Keenan as a director. Keenan had also launched Carmen Electra's career as a film actress in the *Scary Movie* comedy that he produced.

Keenan and I became friends and he admitted being very curious about Prince because he always had such beautiful women around him. Now Keenan was a very tall, good-looking man and I had always had men in my life ask me about Prince, however it surprised me that men in Hollywood like Keenan were even asking. I figured Keenan also knew about me turning Eddie Murphy down for a date since they were friends and this only added to his curiosity.

As I settled back into life in Hollywood, I started studying acting with acclaimed acting coach, Ivanna Chubbuck who was renowned as Brad Pitt's coach. I wanted to become a better actress and have more roles instead of being typecast as the drug dealer's girlfriend or the sexy vixen. During this time in Hollywood, you either did film or television and because I had a strong exotic look, I was doing more film. It would take a few more years before this would change and film actors were doing more television.

Jon Lovitz later asked me if I wanted to attend the VH1 Music Awards with him. He said Prince would be performing. I attended the awards with Jon after we did a commercial shoot for Miller Beer together in Dallas. This was the first time I saw Prince perform with Mayte and I could clearly see they seemed like a perfect match. I was hoping to say hello backstage, but did not see them. However, I did meet Brad Pitt with Jon backstage and this was when he was blond and was doing the film, *Interview With A Vampire*. Brad didn't say much to me because he didn't know my relationship with Jon Lovitz was just friends and seemed enthralled to be meeting Jon.

Soon after this, we had the 1994 earthquake in Los Angeles and I was living in an apartment in Studio City at that time. The home I purchased in Northridge was severely damaged, as that was the earthquake's center. It was hard for me to rent or sell this property during this time. No one wanted to be in Northridge. I had to take out a loan to try and fix the damages and get it rented as soon as possible because I was losing so much money on that property. Ultimately I would later have no choice but to foreclose on that property due to the natural disaster because I owed more on it than it was worth and could not rent or sell it.

I was happy during that time I had decided to take the rest of my money that was in an IRA out early with no penalties, due to the natural disaster and buy another house in Sherman Oaks. I've always followed my intuition and I felt like I didn't want to be in an apartment anymore after that big earthquake. I just felt a house was safer and this would be a smart move to make at that time. I would go on to own that home for eight years and it turned into a great investment that made up for the loss I had on my Northridge home.

I was always entrepreneurial and business minded and had learned a lot about real estate by this time. I knew California real estate was great because most people like myself wanted to come and live in California for the entertainment industry or the weather. I believed in owning a home in California to be a great investment for my future. I was fortunate enough to have worked consistently as a commercial and film actress and I saved up my money to invest in real estate.

By 1993, Prince had changed his name to the symbol and seemed to be making a comeback with his hit, "Most Beautiful Girl In The World." I had lost touch completely due to all the changes in my life and would only think of him if I heard about a concert. He didn't seem to tour much during this period and I didn't hear anything about him being in Los Angeles for a while.

I continued to do other films, such as a comedy, *Busted* with Corey Feldman and Corey Haim. I also did a small role in a film called *A Brilliant Disguise*. However, acting seemed harder than ever and I hated all the driving I was doing even for commercial auditions. I was becoming disenchanted with it all and didn't really know what I wanted. It seemed like the world was changing so rapidly. Everyone was addicted to watching the Menendez brothers' double murder trial on television, and I couldn't help but remember cooking in their kitchen when Prince rented that same house before they killed their parents there.

Prince now had an unpronounceable name and it didn't seem like he kept in touch with anyone from the past. If I were to see him what would I call him? What would I say?

Chapter 13

"Thieves In The Temple"

It was 1994 when I moved from my apartment to my new home in Sherman Oaks, I had my wedding dress and my precious Prince outfits he had given me stored away neatly in a box. Prince's outfits included his matching shoes that matched the material of the pants and we had the same size feet! The bottom of the pant legs had the elastic band that went around the boot heel and the back of the pant was a sheer black lace so you could see through and actually see his butt. These pants were very sexy and fit me like a glove.

The pants matched the jackets which had shoulder pads in them and were designed by Marie France, who did all of the clothing for the *Purple Rain* Tour. Prince had given me a black suit with white buttons, like the one he wore the night we met. He gave me a tan suit embroidered with gold thread in an elaborate pattern, plus a silk paisley, green and gold embroidered suit. All three outfits had matching shoes with the elastic from his pants that went over the heel of the boots. I sometimes wore the outfits - I did a photoshoot with photographer, John Wahlege in Chicago wearing them. I also wore them occasionally to events.

The ruffled poet's shirts had 'Prince' written in purple inside the collar. The sleeves were long, with elastic around the wrist and ruffles that draped over the hands. They had a purple jewel on the elastic. There was even some of his makeup residue on the collar of the shirts and the shirts still smelled of him. I had three of these shirts and loved them so much because they always reminded me of our time together.

Back in 1985 before *Star Search,* when I was still living in Chicago, I decided to donate one suit for auction for The Better Boys Foundation charity. Oprah Winfrey hosted the event before she became a national star for her *Oprah Winfrey Show*. I was dating a guy in Chicago who handled Oprah's money portfolio and he suggested possibly auctioning one of Prince's shirts for this great cause.

The Better Boys Foundation works to fulfill its mission by providing youth with experiences that enhance their emotional, social, academic, and career development. It's their vision that every child - regardless of race, gender, family circumstances or socioeconomic background - will realize the power of his/her potential.

I was always about helping inner city children better their lives. And because I was once one myself, thought I could part with one of my precious shirts for a worthy charity like this. I wore the green paisley outfit to the event and when I walked into the ballroom, Oprah said to me, "You have got the littlest butt I've ever seen; I'm gonna call you, Little Butt." I just laughed and knew she was wondering how on earth I had one of Prince's actual outfits!

We started the bidding at $400 and oddly no one bid on the shirt so I still had it after the auction, which I was secretly happy about. These were items of sentimental value for me and I really didn't want to part with them ever!

Prince also gave me the outfit he wore on the cover of his *Parade* CD and it was also what he wore in his "Kiss" video. This was a two-piece, red pant and cropped top that had white buttons down the side of the pants and down the middle of the top. There were no matching shoes with this outfit.

I think Prince got a kick out of giving me his clothes because they fit me so well and looked great on me. The outfits were very androgynous and could really be worn by a man or woman. We as fans, all know Prince had great style and would go on to change his style to reflect his growth as a man throughout the years. He would write about his unique approach to fashion in a song called "Style" that was on his CD *Emancipation*.

Prince's father was always impeccably dressed in different colored suits during those days and I think Prince had an affinity for doing the same. He loved wearing different colors and everything looked great on him.

Prince had strong input with designers regarding his clothing, which was very important in achieving his unique fashion sense. He had a staff of people at Paisley Park that made his wardrobe in later years.

Sadly, as I prepared to move into my Sherman Oaks home, I discovered my box of Prince outfits has been stolen from me. I desperately went through all my belongings, but they were nowhere to be found. I had them so many years and was just sick that they were gone. I filed a police report and hope that someday they will return to me.

Despite this disappointing start moving into my new home, I settled in and started to love living there. With a new home also came a new love. He was about eleven years older than me, a well-traveled, successful businessman named Seth. We started traveling a lot together and I eventually moved in with him and soon we became engaged. I was finally starting to become happy again in my life.

I had started to read and study spiritual authors such as, Neal Donald Walsh and Wayne Dyer. I felt moved to seek knowledge and to learn as much as I could. It was during this period in my life that I felt I grew the most as a person. I felt blessed to have experienced the amazing journey that brought me thus far and I was ready for more new and wonderful experiences.

I finally was able to forgive myself and let go of my marriage to Randy and filed for divorce. It had been four years of being apart and neither one of us wanted to file for it. It became apparent that holding onto the past was not helping me move forward with my life.

I was no longer a naïve little girl from Baton Rouge, Louisiana. I was a grown woman in her thirties who had been married and divorced. What did I really want in life? I still wanted to be in love and I still wanted that rainbow themed wedding I didn't get with Randy. I didn't want to become jaded and distrustful of others, but I did need to keep my eyes open and be smart.

I thought I was being smart when I began dating Seth - the wealthy businessman who wanted to show me the world that I didn't get to see earlier in life. My dream was to visit Paris, Venice and London again but this time with a man that I loved.

Seth was divorced, in his early forties and had grown up in Beverly Hills. I had never met anyone that knew so much about art, wine and people as Seth. He thought I was a 'diamond in the rough' and wanted to teach me all that he knew about the finer things in life and I was like a sponge for it all, including his business acumen - he was a born salesman.

Seth was also a Prince fan and wanted to know all about my relationship with him.

As I shared some memories with Seth, I began to look into what Prince was doing at that time and discovered his *Emancipation* CD. I could tell he was totally in love from the lyrics he had written for his new bride, Mayte. She seemed perfect for him and together they almost seemed like kids from the same family. It was no surprise that he wrote a song like "Friend, Mother, Sister, Lover, Wife" for her. I was also heartbroken for them when Mayte suffered a miscarriage later that same year and watched the infamous Oprah interview with curiosity. It was perplexing that they would do such an interview so soon after losing their baby.

However, I knew Prince wanted mystery and privacy around his personal life and figured they would try again because you could plainly see how much he loved her. I wanted to feel in love also and felt I was deeply in love with Seth. He treated me like a Princess and took me on the most beautiful trips to all the places of my dreams. Seth also paid for me to find a good therapist and get over my sex issues.

So much of my childhood was stolen because I had to grow up so fast and was so isolated as child. Like Prince, I was also shy and independent as a child. I was a bit of a workaholic and very driven as an adult. And I was impatient and impulsive at times in my life. I had experienced heartache and pain from my divorce and I was now learning to love again and be happy.

I knew the best way to know how Prince was doing in life was to listen to the lyrics of his songs. It was apparent that "Purple Rain" era in the mid-80s was the most magical time in Prince's career and I felt lucky to be a part of that. I would often think back to that time period and wondered if Prince did the same.

It was apparent from the *Emancipation* CD that Prince was happy as 'the symbol' and I was amazed at how good he looked on *Oprah*. He never seemed to age and could still wow the crowd with live performances. I began to hope he would tour so that Seth and I could see him. Perhaps we would begin a new friendship? And I thought he would enjoy meeting Seth. Sometimes we have to be careful what we wish for.

Chapter 14

"1999"

By late 1998, I was engaged to Seth and traveling the world on private yachts and planes.

Prince would soon be in concert at the Hollywood Bowl. Seth explored the layout of the Hollywood Bowl online and got us tickets with second row center seats that cost $500 a piece! We knew how close the stage would be to the front row seats of the Bowl and I surely knew from experience that Prince would see me. This was a time I just wished I had one of his outfits to wear to the concert.

It had been five years since I had last saw him filming the "Diamonds and Pearls" video at Union Station, so I was really excited to see this concert.

I was sitting next to actor, Tom Arnold when the concert started and as usual I was in complete awe of Prince's talent. He had not lost anything over the years and like a fine wine had just gotten even better. Seth was completely amazed as well with his performance.

I kept my eyes focused on him to make eye contact with him throughout the performance, but oddly he never once looked at me. Seth turned to me at one point during the concert and said, "Maybe he doesn't remember you honey?" I was completely surprised that he wasn't looking at me and then suddenly just as he was ending the concert, he said, "I got to have me some dancers up here," and looked straight at me and smiled. I looked at him as if to say, "Are you talking to me?" and he looked back at me smiling and giving me a very knowing look from the past that said, "Yeah Devin, I'm talking to you!"

I was the first one he had come up on stage that night dressed in a sexy black jumpsuit with high heel boots. Many friends like Keenan Ivory Wayans were there that night and saw Prince bring me up on stage first. I knew this was his way of saying hello and could see Seth looking up at us from his seat.

Having several audience attendees come up on stage and dance for the finale number was something Prince included me in many times during his concerts. I knew all I had to do was go backstage at the end and I would be able to have a conversation with him, but I looked down at Seth and felt it wouldn't be right. I knew Prince was married to Mayte and I was engaged to Seth and him having me come up and dance was enough for me. Looking back, I wished I had just gone backstage then. I had no idea the turmoil he was in over the death of his child and with his marriage to Mayte during that time.

Soon after this concert, I received a cassette in the mail at my Beverly Hills mailbox. The handwriting was in purple and the cassette was from Minnesota. There was no note or anything inside except the cassette. The name of the song was called "The War" and it had 'NOT FOR SALE NPG' written on it. I played the song, which was twenty-six minutes in length! The lyrics were very dark and scary. The song lyrics predicted world events that have now transpired and that may also happen in the future.

I learned that this song was given to selected concert ticket holders and has just now in 2016, been released online under Jay Z's new digital download service, Tidal.

The song was a bit disturbing for me and I didn't know what to think of it. I knew he was sending a message and since I had just reconnected with him onstage at the Hollywood Bowl, I wondered exactly what it could be. As usual, there were always more questions than answers regarding Prince.

I had told Seth stories of the Playboy Mansion parties since he lived around the corner from the Playboy Mansion. I was now thirty-five years old and had spent the past five years traveling and living in his world, which was very pampered. Seth had a live-in chef so he didn't need me to cook for him. I lived with him in the same house that the movie *Shampoo* was filmed in. It was one of the most beautiful homes in prestigious Holmby Hills, located just off of Sunset Blvd. I creatively threw some of the best theme parties that had celebrities such as Mick Jagger, Seal and even Hef in attendance. Seth and I were getting quite the reputation around town for throwing some pretty incredible theme parties.

The Playboy Mansion had been dead for several years, due to Hef's marriage to Playmate, Kimberly Conrad. There were seldom parties up there anymore and Hef was raising his two sons, Marston and Cooper with Kimberly during these years. Then suddenly, Kimberly left Hef one New Year's Eve and he was alone in the Mansion after eight years of marriage.

It was also at that time that Hef started to go out to the nightclubs with an entourage of blonds and the Playboy Mansion started to come back to life. Hef was always most comfortable with everyone in Hollywood visiting him at the Mansion. But now he would now go outside of the Mansion to events, parties and nightclubs. The entourage of beautiful blonds became his trademark. And he would bring them with him when he came to the parties Seth and I threw.

At the same time, Hef started his famous parties up once more. It was like he was coming full circle in his life ... in his 70s!

All the stories I had told Seth he discovered for himself as we were on the guest list for the new Playboy parties. It was so fun to experience them, this time with a man I was in love with. When I was a Playmate back in the '80s, we couldn't bring a date to the parties unless they were already a celebrity. The Playmates needed to be approachable at the parties - in many ways it was like work.

Seth threw me a lavish thirty-fifth birthday bash that was a '60s theme because I was born in the '60s and loved that decade's style. I had everyone wear sixties clothing and I dressed up as Cher with a long straight hair wig and a multi colored jumpsuit.

Seth then took me on first class trip to Paris, Bordeaux and St. Tropez. He gave me a beautiful diamond and gold necklace, watch and earring set by designer, Bvlgari. It was the most extravagant jewelry he had ever given me. I felt sure we were going to get married soon. He promised we would just go off on a trip and he would surprise me with a spontaneous wedding and then we would plan my dream wedding afterwards.

We had been together for nearly five years and I kept joking with him that I would be leaving him soon if I didn't get what I wanted. We had a couple of fights over marriage during our five years together and I had given him his ring back a couple of times before and would try and go back to my Sherman Oaks home, but he always would convince me to be patient with him because he had been through a horrible divorce. Seth had one son who was five when we met and was by this time almost ten. His son was split between staying with his father, and then his mother in Beverly Hills.

I loved life with Seth - it brought me opportunities like when we had Hef over for dinner with a few Playmates that I knew well from the '80s - Ava Fabian, Cathy St. George and Julie McCullough. I included on our guest list, Penthouse Pet of The Year icon, Julie Strain who had become a photographer.

That night I said to Hef, "I can't believe I'm entertaining the world's greatest entertainer!" And I thanked him for choosing me as Miss June 1985.

I then gave Hef a tour of Seth's home and this was the only time I had the opportunity to have a real conversation with Hef in all my years associated with *Playboy*. He talked mostly about his love for animals and enjoyed the tour I gave him of Seth's home. He loved the fact that the home was featured in the movie, *Shampoo* because he is such a movie buff.

Hef also attended my thirty-fifth birthday party bash at Seth's home and we were becoming regulars at the Playboy Mansion parties that were quickly becoming the hot ticket to attend again by 1999.

Then tragedy struck.

Soon after my birthday and the lavish European trip Seth had taken me on as a gift, I discovered he had been cheating on me throughout our entire relationship.

I was completely devastated.

The live-in Chef told me all about his infidelity because he grew to despise Seth for it. I confronted Seth and he confessed that he knew he wouldn't have stood a chance with me if I had known what he was really like ... another wannabe Playboy.

Seth could not be faithful and admitted that fact. We broke up.

It was really hard to get past Seth's infidelity because I trusted him more than any man I had ever had in my life. However, because he had given me several years of paid therapy, I was able to understand what happened in my marriage to Randy when I was unfaithful.

My therapist helped me understand that I had never allowed myself to just have spontaneous sex with anyone. And that's what had happened with Marcus' roommate. I always felt I had to be in love to have sex and so what happened with the roommate really confused me, but with the therapist's help I understood the impulses and was able to forgive myself. I applied that same thinking to Seth and decided to forgive him too.

It was also necessary for me to discuss my childhood with the therapist and what Frank did to me so that I could let go of it. I had to learn to allow myself to receive pleasure from sex, which I did not do until I was with Seth. Because of therapy, I was able to understand a lot about myself and today Seth and I are friends.

Since Seth and I were neighbors of the Playboy Mansion and had Hef over for parties, he graciously returned the gesture when the Mansion became popular again around the year 2000. When Seth and I split up, we were both on the guest list for all the future parties. I was again single and for the first time in my life not interested in another relationship. I felt as if I was doomed to never be in one again and vowed that I would be content living alone for the rest of my life.

I felt lost and alone when I moved back to the house I had purchased in Sherman Oaks. I would have to reinvent my life all over again at age thirty-five now. Shortly after my split with Seth, I was rear ended in a car accident by Casey Kasem's daughter, Carrie. This accident caused my right leg to experience hip pain that I still have to this day.

During this recovery period, it was hard for me to wear high heels for photo shoots and I was taking pain pills and felt really depressed. My friend, Julie Strain (Penthouse Pet of the Year and photographer) eventually made me stop taking those pills and after nearly a year, I finally recovered from that accident and my broken heart.

I didn't want to go to the Playboy Mansion parties because I didn't want to see Seth up there. I stopped going to them for over a year and threw myself into reinventing my career.

The Internet was a new way for people to connect and I had seen my friend Cindy Margolis make waves with it. Since I was a consummate homebody, I decided to sell my Sherman Oaks home and move into a larger Studio City home that I could rent for location shoots and also have roommates so that it would pay for itself. I wanted male roommates so that I felt safe living alone, but I did not want a relationship at all. I started back with modeling for Trashy Lingerie and met a younger soft-spoken model named, Dita Von Teese.

Other pinup girls were doing websites during this time and Dita was one of them that I frequently modeled with, along with Julie Strain and a variety of Playmates and Penthouse Pets. These girls were entrepreneurial and were marketing themselves through their websites. I jumped on board and started carving a niche for myself. I had a lot of fans that wondered what happened to me, so I thought I would connect with them directly through the Internet.

During this time, I had the opportunity to go on the *Howard Stern Show*. He had a TV show and a radio show at the time and my appearance was well received, so I went back a second time. It seemed this time Howard was trying to get me to talk about Prince and I really didn't want to, so that one didn't go so well. Howard Stern is nothing like his persona and is actually a very quiet man off the air. He told me he liked me, but I needed to talk more about my personal life, which I just didn't feel comfortable doing at that time.

In 2002, Prince was performing at the Kodak Theater in Hollywood and I was invited to go with my longtime dear friend, Leon Issac Kennedy. It would be a smaller more intimate concert, so I wrote a personal note and put a booklet of my recent modeling photos to give to Prince hoping to see him. I did see Jerome Benton and asked him to give the note to Prince before the concert started. It was clear Prince was trying different things by then and this concert was not what everyone expected. He didn't sing any of his hits and played songs no one had even heard. It was not one of his best performances and both Leon and I were a bit disappointed. I was also disappointed that he didn't respond to my note and photos.

It was during this period of time that Prince was becoming a Jehovah Witness and didn't want to perform any of his old music. He just wasn't the Prince we all expected him to be that night.

It had been over a year since I had gone to a Playboy Mansion party, so I asked Bill Maher if he would go with me to the Midsummer Night's Dream party because I didn't want to go alone. It was strange seeing everyone after not being social for over a year. I think I was somewhat of a mystery to many of my Playboy family friends who didn't really know exactly what was up with me doing a disappearing act like that. Bill told me that night that Steve Fargnoli had passed away of stomach cancer at only fifty-two years old. I felt really sad to hear this news. The fact that Prince and Steve never made up compounded my sadness.

Around 2003, I had an opportunity to see Prince again with one of my roommates who was a big fan. It was during Prince's *Musicology* Tour and I had heard that he would be doing a small private concert at a new nightclub called The Highlands. I noticed he had a girl onstage sitting in a chair and figured it was his second wife, Manuela. It was surprising to me that he married so quickly after he divorced Mayte. Although I was close to the stage in an intimate setting, he did not make eye contact with me that night, but his performance was awesome! Paula Abdul was also at that performance and I spoke with some fans who said they were members of his fan club online. They seemed to know more about what was going on with Prince than anyone. It seemed Prince was utilizing the Internet to promote his music and make a major comeback with tours. He would give away his *Musicology* CD to each person who bought a ticket to the live performance.

We were moving into the 21st century and just as Prince's prophetic lyrics to "The War" chanted, 'the war would go on and on' … 9/11 happened and everything changed.

Chapter 15

"Purple Rain"

As the country found its feet and established a sense of security, 2004 arrived and I was feeling like I wanted to be securely in love again. It had been about five years since my split with Seth. I was now forty-one years old and my life felt somewhat lonely with only my two little Shih-Tzus, Elvis and Romeo. I was somewhat of a recluse who didn't like going to parties and stayed home most weekends teaching my dogs how to sing.

I made my living with my home in rentals for movie location shoots, modeling shoots and did occasional autograph shows around the country to promote myself and my website. Many wealthy older men from the Playboy Mansion were trying to date me during this time, but I didn't feel interested at all in them. I even had some younger guys who tried to date me and I wasn't interested in them either. I was at a point in my life that I would rather be alone than with a man that I wasn't madly in love with. The pain of relationships and trust issues were not worth doing it again otherwise.

While in Kansas on a celebrity autograph show, I saw Playboy Playmate Barbara Moore and actor Lorenzo Lamas there. They were newly engaged and *so* in love. This made me long for that intimacy again with someone. Lorenzo had just become a new cast member on the daytime drama, *The Bold and The Beautiful*. I didn't really know Lorenzo but found him to be a really nice guy who treated Barbara very well.

We happened to be in a limo together on the ride to the airport and Lorenzo said to me, "Devin, you seem like such a nice girl, how come you don't have a man in your life?" I replied, "The old guys are too old and the young guys are too intimidated." He laughed and said, "You need a real man." I laughed and replied, "Yeah, do you know any?"

Lorenzo went on to tell me about a guy he had just befriended on *The Bold and Beautiful* named Winsor Harmon. I knew of this show because I had briefly remembered meeting the lead actor on it, Ronn Moss, back when I first moved to Los Angeles. I secretly wished it was Ronn instead of Winsor, but I knew Ronn had been married for years.

Seemed both Barbara and Lorenzo wanted to set me up on a date after that limo ride. I contemplated meeting Winsor and decided I was ready to start dating again. Over the next couple months, I would run into Lorenzo and Barbara at parties and other events and Lorenzo would always remind me that he had not forgotten me and that he just had not seen Winsor because he wasn't working as much on the show.

Then one day I had a message on my answering machine with both Barbara and Lorenzo's voices asking me if I could meet them at the restaurant, Mastros. Barbara continued, "We're going to introduce you to Ronn Moss."

To be honest, I thought (because she's the epitome of the blonde Barbie doll in appearance) that she was having a 'blonde moment' because I never heard Ronn's name come out of Lorenzo's mouth. He was always mentioning Winsor to me. Ronn was only in my head and I never verbalized it to them. I got dressed to meet Barbara and Lorenzo for dinner, I thought I would be meeting Winsor for the first time.

However, when I arrived at Mastros, it was indeed Ronn Moss who was sitting at the bar looking directly at me as I walked through the door! I quickly looked away thinking, "Why is he here, he's only been in my head?" I turned to look at Ronn and our eyes met, so I walked over to him and said, "I thought I was meeting Winsor?" He replied, "Winsor is married." I was a bit puzzled and he continued, "I'm divorced." I looked up to the heavens and in my head said, "Thank you God."

Suddenly, I felt excited and started asking Ronn if he remembered meeting me back in the early 1987. I had gone to a wrap party of a movie that Ronn's (now ex) wife and Joey Gian had done together called *Mad About You*. It was written and directed by a mutual friend named, Lorenzo Doumani. Ronn remembered Lorenzo introducing us at that wrap party. Ronn had just got a role on the new daytime drama, *The Bold and The Beautiful* and I had just won *Star Search*. Neither of us had seen Lorenzo in ten years, but we remembered that night. I remembered Ronn told me had been a musician before *B & B*, he was a member of the group Player known for their hit, "Baby Come Back." That song was a favorite during my high school days, so I was totally impressed that someone as handsome, nice and talented as Ronn had achieved so much. We continued our conversation hitting it off instantly as Barbara and Lorenzo joined us.

We were taken to our table and sitting at the table next to us was the writer, director of the movie our exes had done together, Lorenzo Doumani! Having not seen him in over a decade, he was just as surprised to see us! I took this as a big omen that something was just right about this date.

Ronn and I talked most of the evening and he was a complete gentleman opening the door for me and very charming and respectful. He didn't even try to kiss me goodnight. I could feel that something was happening and felt excited to see him again.

I later learned that Lorenzo Lamas had told Winsor about me and Winsor revealed he was married, something Lorenzo didn't know because he was newly on the show. It was Winsor who suggested Lorenzo introduce me to Ronn. All I know is I was forever grateful that fate transpired this way because Ronn had most of the qualities I wanted in a man during this time of my life.

Ronn was a bit older, but looked great and was very fit for a man in his early fifties. He was very creative, something I craved because I'm that way. He had a wonderful sense of humor, was very intelligent and he was already a father to two little girls, aged five and ten years old. I always wondered if I could even have children and being in my forties didn't think it would be possible. I was totally okay with a man who had children already. I didn't mind being stepmom.

Growing up in and out of foster homes, made me want to give to children of any kind. I had volunteered to be a big sister to a foster child at the foster home that Marilyn Monroe grew up in called Hollygrove. The thought of two adorable little girls thrilled me.

Divorce is always hardest on the children and I remembered Randy saying how great he felt that his parents and step-parents got along. I also knew that Prince didn't like his parent's divorce and it affected him greatly. I had a lot of compassion for Ronn's children. However, I wasn't quite comfortable with another situation that I soon learned about.

Ronn lived with his ex-mother-in-law and referred to his ex-wife's family in the present tense when introducing me to them. It made me feel like we were having an affair - but he had been divorced for over two years! I didn't think this was a good situation and it felt uncomfortable, especially around the holidays, which were spent with his ex-wife's family. He explained that they had been in his life for sixteen years and were part of his children's lives and had sided with him during his divorce, which was very unusual.

I tried to understand, but this situation was very odd. So Ronn and his kids spent a lot of time at my house. I had a pool and they loved to come swim. I enjoyed cooking for them and they seemed to love my cooking. We would also spend quite a bit of time visiting Winsor and hung out with Lorenzo Lamas' children also.

As great as Ronn was during this time, he still had a lot of residual anger about his divorce. He had been working for nearly twenty years on *The Bold and The Beautiful* and his ex-wife and taxes ate most of his money. Unlike Lorenzo Lamas, Ronn worked almost every day on the show because he was a worldwide star in his role as Ridge Forrester. The show was one of the biggest soaps in the world.

Ronn seemed a bit lost when we met and reminded me of myself after my relationship with Seth ended. He seemed like he didn't know where he belonged. I wanted to help him get out of the funk he was in and move forward in his life. I could see he lacked balance in many areas of his life. I knew that sometimes life throws you curve balls so that you can grow and learn. I really learned a lot being totally alone and not in a relationship during the years after Seth. I wanted to help Ronn get his life back in balance by offering what I had learned in that time.

I found out by looking at Ronn's resume that he was in the movie, *Hot Child In The City*. This was the movie I got my SAG card on! Ronn told me that he met his now ex-wife on this movie. I couldn't believe a coincidence this big was between us and having never seen the movie, I became curious to see it. While watching it, I saw myself for a few seconds dressed in that white outfit that I wore to Tramp the night the cigar-smoking Hollywood producer told me he was going to put me in his movie.

Watching the movie, it was revealed that I got my SAG card saying "Hi" to Ronn in that movie, and yet we both were never introduced to each other off the set. In the film, Ronn was preparing for a fight scene and sitting at the bar of a nightclub. The cameras were rolling and the director said to me, "Devin, just walk past that guy and say hi, and you'll have your SAG card." I did as I was told!

In another scene, I danced in a nightclub with Ronn's now ex-wife! These were all such weird coincidences.

Ronn lived in the home he grew up in with his two daughters, Creason who was ten years old and Calee who was five, when we started dating. They seemed very attached to their daddy and would sleep with him, along with their cat, Nero. His ex-wife was living with her boyfriend and the children were split fifty-fifty between both parents. So Ronn would get up very early to make his children breakfast and lunches and take them to school, before going to CBS studios in Hollywood to film *B & B*.

I lived in my home in Studio City and thought getting involved romantically would not go very far with Ronn, given his situation. I knew I would not want to move into his home that he had shared with his ex-wife ... and now his ex-mother-in-law. And I didn't think he would ever want to move into my place.

Creason his oldest, had expressed how much she loved horses and Ronn told me how much he wanted to live in a horse community with acreage around him. He had lived in Hollywood his entire life and was tired of barking dogs and constant traffic.

The Moss family shared a great love for horses because Ronn's mother loved riding and even taught Elizabeth Taylor how to ride for her movie, *National Velvet*. Ronn spoke fondly of his mother who died when he was only 18 years old. He was happy that Creason had inherited the passion he also shared for horses.

One day I discovered a horse community called Santa Rosa Valley in a *Homes & Land* real estate magazine. I convinced Ronn to take a look at a few homes in that area, which was about forty-five minutes north of Hollywood. He ultimately fell in love with a six-acre home, on which he could build a barn and have horses. It was clear that this family needed a fresh start to move forward and I was happy to help them. I knew from experience that it would be a necessity for his wellbeing and to continue on with his life after being hurt in his divorce. I was using what I had learned through my break ups to help him find balance in his life.

I could also see that he needed a mortgage to offset some of the taxes he was paying out each year. I helped him buy the property and even went on to pick out furniture and help decorate the girls' rooms. But mostly I worked to help him get his life organized.

It was during this time that our relationship took a turn to a deeper level and I began spending most weekends with him and the kids at their new home. It seemed as though we had moved from being friends to being more of a couple. But Ronn worked constantly and would often travel to Europe and Australia for commercial, movie and concert gigs.

In late 2005, Ronn invited me to join him when he shot a juice commercial in Melbourne, Australia. I had never experienced that country and was thrilled to join him. It was obvious that the people in Australia adored Ronn and I found the Aussies to be quite nice and laid back.

When we returned to Los Angeles, Ronn and I were starting to get even closer. We discussed a lot of things and realized we had a lot in common. He was a terrific musician and expressed how much he wanted to meet a musician like Prince. I began to contemplate reconnecting with Prince so that Ronn could meet him.

I soon discovered Ronn had not even seen *Purple Rain* and actually wasn't a major fan but had become more curious about Prince because of my history. However, being a musician himself, he really respected Prince as a musician and wanted very much to see him in concert. I wanted very much for Ronn to meet Prince and hoped that would transpire one day.

Chapter 16

"When Doves Cry"

As my romantic relationship developed with Ronn, it became apparent that we would have to sell either my house or his house if we were going to live together. He was just too busy to build a barn as he had dreamed for Creason to have horses. The house he had purchased was perfect for them, but he didn't think it would be big enough for me to move in with him.

I was beginning to feel like I didn't know where I lived anymore because I had some clothes at Ronn's new house and he would want to spend most weekends there. It was not a comfortable feeling for me also because Ronn was not in a marriage frame of mind. He was actually very anti-marriage due to his horrible divorce. I had vowed never to move into another guy's home after what happened with Seth and so we would need to buy a home together to move forward as a couple.

One day as we were hiking and talking about our hopes and dreams, he asked me how I liked Santa Rosa Valley. I could tell he was wanting to live together somehow and I had no objections to it. Our relationship was going along nicely, although I wasn't thrilled he was so anti-marriage. We spoke of what we both wanted in a home and I thought perhaps I could start looking for that dream home and we could sell his homes and start a new life together.

I started looking around and found a great home that seemed perfect for a growing family and it had a barn for horses! It would however take selling one of our homes to get it. I believe in 'where there is a will there is a way' and against the odds we managed to get this home and refinance all our other mortgages on our other homes, managing to rent them. However, we did not anticipate the great real estate depression that started soon after we purchased our home.

Home values dropped drastically and all we could hope for was to keep these houses rented until we could sell them. I had been dealing with tenants and real estate for years, so I decided to get my real estate license and continue to deal with these properties. I also helped Ronn with picking up the girls from school on days he couldn't do so, due to his long hours on the set. I managed his home and helped him keep organized in his life.

Slowly life began to get balanced and Ronn and the kids seemed very content and happy. There were lots of other kids around their age in our little horse community and Creason had her dream - a horse named, Dante. My life was very busy as I found myself managing all our properties, but also helping Ronn raise his two daughters, as well as, handling all our finances.

It took a lot of work to get things back in balance for Ronn, but it helped me know that Ronn was clearly my soul mate.

Ronn proposed to me with a beautiful, five carat, yellow diamond for my forty-fifth birthday in 2008 to my surprise! He knew it was something I always wanted and the one thing that Seth never gave me. He also understood how important it was for me to feel connected to being part of a family. We started planning that rainbow outdoor wedding I always dreamed of for the fall of 2009.

On September 25, 2009, Ronn and I finally married after five years of courtship. I got that rainbow outdoor wedding of my dreams and included Creason and Calee as bridesmaids. Despite the horrible Californian brush fires that almost caused our venue, the Moorpark Country Club, to cancel us, we had a gorgeous wedding day that included one hundred friends and family members. We even included Prince in our wedding when we danced our first dance as husband and wife to his song, "Kiss."

Two weeks after my wedding, I had to go to the hospital in an emergency because I was hemorrhaging blood. I had been experiencing increasingly painful periods. The doctors told me what I knew intuitively, that I would need to eventually have a hysterectomy like my mother. I was so grateful to have Ronn by my side during this crisis.

When I was feeling healthier, I heard Prince was on tour with Chaka Khan. Ronn and I looked for the best tickets online that we could find, but they were terribly expensive. He was playing at the Staples Center in Los Angeles and I picked out seats close to the stage so he could see me like he did at the Hollywood Bowl.

We went with our neighbors who rented a limo and we were all looking forward to an amazing evening. When we arrived, I was shocked to see that we front row seats to the back of the stage that was set up very high. It was awful and I was pissed that we had spent $2,000 for these kinds of tickets!

The stage was set up in the shape of his symbol and he played most of the concert on the other side, so we hardly got to see him! The sound was way too loud and the venue was not set up in the way I had seen the *Purple Rain* concerts so many times. Needless to say, I was completely disappointed in that concert and unfortunately, that was the last time I went to see him perform. Ronn and I were hoping to see Prince in a more intimate setting the next time he was to come to Los Angeles, but we didn't hear of any more shows like that.

Prince did seem to do more television than ever before at this time and I recall watching that awesome Super Bowl performance he did in the rain and his incredible Rock and Roll Hall of Fame induction guitar solo on "My Guitar Gently Weeps" in 2004. But Prince was not performing live in concert quite as much as he use to and I heard he was living in Toronto with his second wife, Manuela.

Looking back, I don't know why I didn't think to try and call Paisley Park during this time and connect with Prince personally? I was just used to him reaching out to me through Playboy if he wanted to get in touch with me.

Old friends, who were major Prince fans and knew him like, DJ Michael Creamer, would call me if Prince had a concert going on in Los Angeles. Mike Creamer (many stars called him "Stereo Mike") did all the car and home stereo installation for major stars like Prince, Michael Jackson, Quincy Jones, Vanity ... and me.

Michael knew Prince very well and adored him as an artist and performer, so if Prince were anywhere nearby, we would have heard about it. But, in the past few years at the time of writing this, it didn't seem like Prince was performing much at all around Los Angeles.

Then last year (2015) Ronn and I heard about his *Piano & A Microphone* Tour and we were looking forward to that and planned on getting tickets when he would play LA.

Denise Matthews, aka Vanity passed away on Feb 15, 2016 and I felt a very strong sadness. I knew that Vanity had become an Evangelist and had been battling a kidney illness due to drug abuse for many years. Her death really affected me because it would hit home for anyone who was in Prince's circle.

Denise was a part of Prince's early roots. If you wondered why Prince chose women who looked so similar all you had to do was look at Vanity – he saw himself in her. Prince changed her name from Denise to Vanity, and he developed *Purple Rain* as a vehicle to make them both major stars.

Crossover mainstream stardom was something both Prince and Vanity wanted badly in the mid '80s. The part Apollonia played was written for Vanity initially, but Vanity and Prince broke up and Vanity left him before shooting began on *Purple Rain*. Steve Fargnoli told me how he had to scout through tons of cattle calls to find a girl with the right look and height to replace Vanity for the movie. Steve said he wished he had met me a year earlier because it could have been me in that role.

Vanity's death triggered me to look up her ministry on YouTube and I saw a completely different woman than the woman who oozed sex so much back in the day. Denise the Evangelist had transformed in a beautiful angelic soul who seemed to be a sweet and happy person that I wished I could have known.

I had a Toronto journalist reach out to me for an interview, shortly after her death because I posted my condolences to her sister, Patricia on my Facebook page. I felt sad for her passing at such a young age and my mind immediately went to Prince.

I wondered how he was taking this news and since I've always been intuitive, I felt he was very depressed and sad over it. I said this to Ronn and continued to feel it strongly in my soul. I also kept telling Ronn that I felt something really big was about to happen.

Ironically, I got a text from a mutual friend inviting me to Denise's funeral outside of San Francisco. I was told that Prince may attend the services and that he was performing in Oakland.

I would have liked to attend, but Ronn was performing with Player in Palm Springs that day. I noticed that Apollonia had posted a very loving post on her Facebook about Denise's service and said that they had gone to see Prince perform afterwards. She went on to say how Prince took the time to look at baby photos of Apollonia 6 members Brenda and Susan Moonsie's children. There seemed to be a lot of sentimental energy coming all of a sudden from Prince to people from his past, something that was unusual for him.

The past six months before Prince's death, his name had been coming up a lot for me. It started in Belgium in October 2015 when Ronn met with a music promoter to discuss a possible European tour. It turned out this man named Stanny was already working with Prince on his tours and told us wonderful stories of their working relationship. I laughed and asked Stanny to say hello to Prince from me, and to tell him I wanted some more of his clothes.

A couple of months later, I was working on *The Bay*, the drama series that Ronn and I produce and he acts on. Actress, Terri Ivens was doing a scene with Ronn and mentioned out of the blue that she had dated Prince in the early '90s when he was 'the symbol.' I had no idea she even knew him. Terri told me she met Prince when he picked her out of the audience at one of his concerts when he was 'the symbol.' She said she hung out with him a few times, but didn't sleep with him.

Then a very strange thing happened. I had a spa day set in Studio City with my longtime girlfriend, Kira. The woman giving me my facial was a peppy young lady with red hair who said she was from Minneapolis. I mentioned I had been there because of Prince and she looked at me as said, "Well you are his type," and told me her sister dated Prince in the mid '90s. Then she proceeded to show me a photo of her sister who looked like she could be my sister! I mean what are the odds?

Over the past thirty years, I had heard many stories of Prince's dark side and figured this was the side he said I could never see of him. I took a lot of what was told to me over the years with a grain of salt and knew Prince was an enigma that many people tried to figure out, including myself. Now yet another coincidence was giving me information out of the blue about Prince. I felt it was a message and came home and shared this with Ronn, telling him I had a feeling that something was not well with Prince.

All the serendipity around Prince had me wondering what it could mean. At first I thought, perhaps we were going to see him in concert for his *Piano & A Microphone* Tour. Then I had this feeling of dread come over me and I kept telling Ronn that I didn't think Prince was well. Thoughts of his baby with Mayte that died crossed my mind. Then my mind spiraled into more panic. Did he have a split personality and show different sides of himself to different people? Was he leading a double life?

There were as usual, more questions than answers when it came to Prince. All I knew was that he was on my mind a lot and I felt concerned for him.

On the morning of April 21, 2016, I was texting my girlfriend Tina, who happens to be from Minneapolis and was Prince's neighbor many years ago. Tina was also a good friend with Bobby Z and his wife, Vicki. Bobby Z was Prince's drummer in the Revolution. Tina told me someone had died at Prince's house but she didn't know who it was.

Soon afterwards, another friend texted me saying how sorry she was about Prince. I asked, "What do you mean, what's wrong with Prince?" And she said he had passed away. At first I didn't believe it was real and thought it was an Internet hoax, but she said it was all over the news. I quickly checked online for myself and was completely devastated. Tears started pouring down my face. I was in utter shock. It just couldn't be true. He couldn't be gone?

Prince had that otherworldly quality about him that made him seem like he would live forever. His energy was always so high and he took excellent care of himself. I never saw him do drugs or drink much, except a bit of red wine. He was way too controlling and way too driven as a musician to be out of control with drugs or alcohol and didn't tolerate it from others around him. Prince was the consummate perfectionist and control freak. It just wasn't his style to be a drug addict and out of control.

He did say to me there was a side to him that I could never see and I never did see this side, but others who knew him had. The dark side was not drug abuse, it was the controlling demeanor he had for those who worked with him and those who were romantically involved with him. Shelia E shared in her book, *The Beat of My Own Drum* that he wouldn't let her attend her grandmother's funeral.

235

Prince was such a perfectionist that he expected the same from everyone around him. He could also be insensitive to other people having their own lives and demanded they work on holidays such as Christmas and New Year's Eve, if he decided he wanted to record or rehearse. Prince expected you to devote your time to him whenever he required it, if you worked for him.

It was a little too much for most people and ultimately is why most people left him, even lovers. He could wear a person out with his controlling nature. I may have been one of the few people in his life that did not see that dark side and I think that's why he ended things the way he did with me.

He only wanted to show me the good side of him.

Chapter 17

"Nothing Compares To You"

Prince's death just didn't seem real, but the press about it was indeed very real. I couldn't stop crying and felt a wave of emotions engulf me throughout the day. Many longtime friends and people I hadn't heard from in years were texting, calling and sending me messages of condolences. This felt like one of my premonition dreams, except it was reality.

I had several press people contacting me for interviews, but I just didn't feel like talking. This actually made me laugh, because I thought Prince would be laughing at the fact that I didn't feel like talking! He always thought I was way more talkative than him. But, all I could do was think of past memories and at the fact that I would never get to see him again, nor introduce him to Ronn. I felt bad that I never reached out to him over the years. It made me appreciate my memories even more.

The weekend after his death, I did not sleep well and felt so incredibly sad. I kept saying to Ronn that I felt he had taken too many pain pills by accident. I could totally see him losing track of time, not sleeping and perhaps taking too many that stopped his heart.

The Monday following his death, my friend Tina woke me up by calling and saying that *People* Magazine wanted to speak with me about Prince and that they were doing a tribute. She recommended that they talk to me because she thought I had such a beautiful story. I really couldn't think straight at that time and had not been sleeping well, but agreed to tell them only how we met. I didn't feel like getting too deep in conversation.

There seemed to be non- stop tributes on television and lots of speculation over how he died on a daily basis. The one song that many people seemed to gravitate to was "Nothing Compares 2 U." It seemed to sum Prince up the most because no one compared to him. It would be hard to see any other performer doing those high falsettos and singing "When Doves Cry" or "Let's Go Crazy."

Prince left his mark on this world in many ways. He influenced fashion, pioneered alternative ways for an artist to distribute their music and showed off his artistic marketing skills by releasing a wide variety of music, his way.

In the aftermath of his death he dominated the R&B, Pop and Rock Billboard charts, breaking even the Beatles record. The movie, *Purple Rain* was re-released in theaters and a whole new generation was bingeing on everything Prince.

Prince was said to not have a will in place and the Internet was dominated by all kinds of T-shirts, necklaces and Prince memorabilia for sale. I just refused to believe that a man as intelligent as Prince did not have a will and told Ronn that I believed he had it in the vault. Prince kept all his personal things and unreleased music that he did daily in a big bank vault at Paisley Park. Only he had the code to open this vault. Soon we read that authorities were drilling the famous vault open. I figured we would hear that a video will would be found soon and he might have even left us with one more, never before seen, performance.

In the meantime, his remaining half siblings and one full blood sister were fighting over his estate, said to be worth around $300 million. Prince had battled Warner Brothers for his masters and he had signed a $100 million deal with them a couple years ago. He had proven that he could sell out high priced concert tickets in a matter of minutes and was now marketing himself with lots of TV appearances. I think it was safe to say Prince was going to be worth even more money dead than alive.

There was a lot of mystery surrounding his death when he was discovered in the elevator of Paisley Park on the morning of April 21, 2016. The press had reported that Prince was battling an ongoing flu and his private plane had to make an emergency landing in Illinois days before his untimely death, where paramedics had to give him a 'save' shot against opiates in his body.

The speculation was that Prince may have died of an overdose of Percocet due to pain in his hips from dancing in his high heels so many years. There were also conspiracy theories that Prince was murdered by the Illuminati because he was starting to speak out about chemtrails and the New World Order that was starting to overtake us all. It was reported he predicted 9/11 in one of his concerts back in 1999. Hearing this I remembered that song, "The War" that predicted dark times to come.

After Prince's death, we learned how much he gave anonymously to humanitarian causes that benefited children's education and environmental issues. It seemed Prince was focused on trying to make our world a better place. It was also rumored he was without a girlfriend and celibate, which would be a first for him. There was also speculation that he may have had AIDS, which I found hard to believe. Contrary to the belief of some, Prince was not gay and I couldn't imagine him using a needle.

Prince dominated the press for weeks after his death and was trending daily online. Many people noted that his last Instagram post stated, "Just when you thought it was safe." He added to the mystery by telling his last concert audience just days before he died, "Wait a few days before wasting any prayers," as many were concerned after hearing about that emergency private plane landing and the 'save' shot he received. Yet some local people in Minneapolis saw him riding his bike around a couple days before he died as though nothing was wrong at all.

Chapter 18

"Pop Life"

The lyrics to some of Prince's earlier songs like "Pop Life," state clearly what he thought of drugs, "Whatcha putting in your nose, is that where your money goes?"

It was obvious that Prince was not in support of drugs and he was always advising kids to stay in school. He was very aware that his fans now had kids and he wanted to be good role model for them. Prince did not abuse his body going so far as to became vegan, eating a healthy meatless, junk food free diet later in life, which was very different to the way he ate when I was with him. It was a hard pill to swallow (pardon the pun) that he would die of an opioid overdose.

It was interesting, in this year of Prince's death, that pop mega star, Madonna, was chosen to sing the Prince tribute with Stevie Wonder at the Grammy Awards. When he and I were dating, I had asked Prince what he thought of her and he said, "I don't like blondes and she is a very calculating woman, Devin." I don't know whether he would have been thrilled she sang his song, but I'm sure he was thrilled Stevie Wonder did.

But Madonna is a megastar and her appearance was likely chosen by the producers as appropriate to honor the megastar that Prince was – well, still is.

During Prince's rise to stardom, he was often compared to another megastar, Michael Jackson. I think it flattered him because Prince had great admiration for Michael, how could he not? He grew up watching Michael as a kid just like we all did. However, at the same time he was a bit bugged by the constant comparisons. I remembered when Michael won several Grammys and Prince and I were in his purple limousine.

Prince was imitating Michael's high-pitched voice and making fun of him. I couldn't believe he was doing that and told him not to make fun of Michael! He responded by saying, "Well he doesn't write his songs and play a bunch of different instruments like I do." He knew that was their big difference; however deep inside, he was flattered to be compared to such a great artist as Michael Jackson.

It was sad that Michael Jackson didn't really have a childhood and was often misunderstood by the press because he seemed to relate more to children. I knew many people who grew up with Michael. They were emphatic he was not a pedophile and was just trying to have the childhood that he never had, because he was always performing, working and traveling as a child. Michael had a big family with lots of brothers and sisters and a very controlling dad, who pushed him to perfection as an entertainer.   It was an extremely difficult environment for a child to grow up in.

Prince did have a childhood and from what I understood, was doted on by his parents because he was so cute. But, his parents divorced when he was ten years old and this affected him greatly. Prince had many half siblings that he was not close to because they were much older. However, he idolized his dad who was a musician and wanted to be a musician from an early age just like him. Unlike Michael, Prince was self-motivated and he did not need to be pushed to perfection, he strived for it daily.

Prince would go on to continue to write and produce hundreds, if not thousands of songs that are locked away in a bank vault for future generations to hear. The comparisons between Michael Jackson and Prince will continue for years for many reasons. They both are without a doubt, two of the world's most talented performers. And both were just so awesome to watch in concert. They both could sing and dance and they both had an otherworldly presence that was bigger than life. Prince and Michael Jackson were ironically both the same age when they died in equally tragic circumstances.

I think Michael and Prince both respected each other greatly, but there was likely a lot of competitiveness between them.

Prince's life will be studied through his music and the lyrics he wrote during specific time periods. I believe he planned it that way and wanted the fans to learn about him through the music. Prince also wanted Paisley Park to be like Graceland was to Elvis. It has its own rehearsal hall, nightclub and mega recording studio, so that it could be his playground on a daily basis. Over the years he collaborated there with people he idolized, as well as those who idolized him: Lenny Kravitz, Beyoncé, Alicia Keys, Tevin Campbell and George Clinton - just to name a few. He wanted it to become a place fans could visit in the future and learn about him and his music. Just as Elvis died at Graceland, Prince died at Paisley Park.

His spirit will always be a part of that place.

Chapter 19

"Controversy"

Controversy was the title of Prince's album that was released in October, 1981 and it was the same month and year I experienced the most controversy in my life – my first appearance in *Playboy*.

Prince was booed off stage when he opened for the Rolling Stones' concert in Los Angeles that month too, so this was a pivotal time in his career that added to his desire to rise above the people that didn't understand him and express his art even more defiantly.

Controversy had songs that focused on society, government, war, politics, as well as his favorite subject - sex. The title song "Controversy" spoke volumes as to who Prince was at the time and what he was all about. Surprisingly, he included the Lord's Prayer in the middle of the song - maybe he was looking for redemption even back then, long before it became the focus of his life as a Jehovah's Witness.

Controversy has always surrounded Prince in life, so it's of no surprise that it would be the case in death. While the public awaited the autopsy report, there were all kinds of speculation to how Prince died – just as there was when Michael Jackson died ironically on June 25th, which is my birthday.

My intuition that Prince had succumbed to an accidental overdose of painkillers was sadly proved correct.

I think Prince and I were alike in the way we thought of drugs. I personally never smoked pot until I was in my early 30s and it was because it relaxed my horrible period cramps. I hate drugs and never wanted to ever be dependent on a pain pill or any pharmaceutical drug. I watched my mother take over thirty-five different pills during the last year of her life as she battled breast cancer.

Knowing Prince and his mind and temperament, he just didn't want to deal with physical pain and would probably do (or take) whatever it took to not feel it - because all that man wanted to do most of time was play music. How can you concentrate on playing music if you are in pain?

Legal, doctor-prescribed drugs got Prince addicted and he could not control the necessary increasing dosage to sustain masking the pain. He was too private to want anyone to know his struggle, so he would surely have dealt with that on his own, until he couldn't any longer. Leading to this heartbreaking outcome.

It was revealed in the final autopsy report that Prince had no other health issue. He did not have AIDS or HIV as the press was speculating, but he did weigh only 112lbs at death. I have personally seen another person dear to me, shrink down to nothing and eventually die due to pain pill addiction, just like this and it's very sad. I believe these pharmaceutical companies who get these doctors to prescribe these addictive drugs are no better than a pusher on the street giving a 'fix' to someone who is addicted to crack-cocaine like Vanity was. The difference is that it's doctor-prescribed, so it must be okay? Didn't we see the same thing with Elvis Presley and Michael Jackson? Then the patient overdoses and no one wants to admit blame.

Prince was not into drugs and probably hated the fact that he had to take anything to keep from feeling his physical pain. I'm sure all that did was get him in a bad mood and Prince loved being in a good mood. He loved life, loved throwing parties, dancing, having other amazing musicians to play with him. He lived for those moments in life every minute of every day.

Prince did not believe in celebrating birthdays. He said, "People should be nice to one another every day." He didn't care about time and didn't do things according to a schedule. I would not be surprised if he forgot that he had taken a pill and unwittingly took another one. These kinds of pills are very dangerous for anyone to be taking and in my opinion should not even be prescribed by doctors.

Prince would be a stubborn, hard to deal with patient, in my opinion. Because he is so controlling, he may have been told the risks involved with this pain reliever, but opted for it anyway.

Many friends could attest he never showed interest in recreational drugs and if he has dabbled in anything it would be the same things most of us have dabbled in. Does that make you a drug addict if you experiment with something and realize you never want to do that again? I know I did this very thing with cocaine and hated it! I think cocaine is a stupid drug and hated the edgy feeling I had and the feeling in my throat. I tried it once and never did it again.

However, I like to smoke pot on occasion and don't feel any kind of addiction. I actually, eat, sleep and feel more relaxed smoking pot than drinking alcohol. I'm quite sure Prince probably dabbled in smoking pot during his life and maybe even trying cocaine, but was he the type to do hard drugs repeatedly? No.

The final autopsy report showed that Prince did die of an overdose of an opiate called, Fentanyl, a drug that is more powerful than morphine or Percocet. It was said that this overdose was accidental. My instinct was proven correct.

Prince was seen picking up a prescription from the Walgreen's the night the day before he died, wearing a black outfit, the same outfit he was wearing when he was found dead in the elevator. It is so sad.

The fact that Fentanyl is a very potent, very addictive drug, which is sold on the streets and called China Girl, The Bomb and Murder, says it all.

I think as Prince aged, his chronic pain kicked in from all the wear and tear on his body. Years of dancing in high heels and doing splits, jumps and spins onstage had to take its toll on his hips.

Rumors of double hip surgery emerged and we saw Prince with a cane for a while. We didn't know if it was part of his fashion statement or if it was needed because of his hips? As usual, fans always speculated with more questions than answers. Like for most people recovering from surgery of this kind, doctors prescribe strong painkillers.

Patients like Prince who have a strong work ethic and a very successful life are the prime patients that will be attracted and become addicted to an opiate. They want to be pain free and continue to create their livelihood. The doctors see them as cash cows.

The tragedy of Prince's death has thrust the drug, Fentanyl in the limelight now, just as Propanol was discussed in the press after Michael Jackson's death. The fact that rock stars and people who have a lot of money in general, can have access to pharmaceutical drugs that are this deadly, speaks volumes. It's almost as if doctors are giving them a death sentence. These drugs are deadly if dosage is not monitored properly.

I know from my own experience, having surgery for a hysterectomy in 2014, when I was given Percocet for pain, I didn't want to take it. Ronn and I both shy away from any prescribed drugs because we don't trust them. I highly recommend watching the movie, *Side Effects* as a great example of how some drugs can turn anyone's life upside down.

Prince was the epitome of clean and healthy living for the majority of his life. It's a very sad ending to a life so bright and beautiful. It didn't have to happen. This should be a wake-up call folks!

It makes me angry that the government and pharmaceutical companies are making so much money off of these drugs! It was reported that this drug, Fentanyl has killed more people 'accidentally' than any other drug! It's as though we are giving these companies permission to kill us!

I think back to all the pills I watched my mother take in the last months of her short life. She battled breast cancer and went through chemo and while she was a hospice patient she still was prescribed over thirty pills a day! Why do we have to take all these pills? I believe the pharmaceutical companies want us to think we have to take as many pills as possible, for just about any aliment. It makes them lots of money.

I know a girl who sells pharmaceuticals to doctors. Her job is selling new pills to various doctors so that they will prescribe these to their patients instead of, or even *in addition*, to other ones. She gives doctors all kinds of incentives to buy and prescribe more pills to patients. She keeps the doctors supplied with the newest drugs on the market. Isn't that the same as a drug dealer on the street?

It's so very sad that Prince's life had to end so tragically and now puts him as a poster child for the growing awareness of the 'over-prescribed' epidemic.

As much of a mystery in life, Prince will now also be in death. His story is one for the history books indeed. I'm just happy I was part of that amazing history with him - my only wish now is that his soul is resting in peace with his father, mother and child.

I want to address one final bit of 'controversy.' Many men have asked me, "Would you have been as attracted to him if he wasn't a rock star?" The answer is yes, because Prince's soul was so in touch with both his feminine and masculine side and that's why he attracted so many women.

If you've noticed, women love to dress well, smell good, look great and be seductive. Prince knew how to do that also and even admitted that he felt he had an alter ego named Camille. He was a true Gemini. He had a dual personality that he showed to different people. He even wrote songs under the name, Camille and created a higher voice for his alter ego on songs like, "If I Were Your Girlfriend."

Prince also had a very masculine side to him, the one that was charming, romantic and funny. This was the one that was also controlling and bit jealous and possessive with his girlfriends. The combo of both these personalities made Prince so uniquely different. Women couldn't help but be attracted. We as women love that combo and then if they are good in bed - you are surely hooked.

Prince may have been small in height, but he lacked nothing in the bedroom. He was gentle, romantic and sweet, but could also be sexy and dirty, without being too rough. What more does a girl need? He was always highly energetic and fun to be around.

He had a hard time trusting people and thought the only way he could trust them was if they were on his payroll. Most people wanted something from him. When you are that big of a celebrity, it becomes hard to really see who your true friends are. People get jealous, some become competitive and some just want to take advantage.

I'm sure you can imagine the things Prince had to endure in his world, just being Prince. The controversy of who he truly was will always exist, because he was different things to different people. He showed different sides of himself to you depending on who you were. I think he chose to show me only the good side of him because that's the way he wanted me to remember him.

That's what he really was in the end, a good person with a bad addiction.

Chapter 20

"Sometimes It Snows In April"

I visited Prince in Minneapolis in April 1985 and I remember that he was excited to play his new song, "Sometimes It Snows In April" on the piano for me. He knew I loved the softer side of him and he always gravitated to playing something pretty for me when we were together. I remember the song making me cry - I thought it was so beautiful. He told me the song was for his movie, *Under the Cherry Moon*, and it was based on his character, Christopher Tracy. The lyrics told of his character dying and spoke of how love was everlasting. It was not a typical song for Prince at the time.

Toward the end of Prince's life, he was showing us that he had grown and transformed himself from the Prince we once knew - and from 'the symbol' - into a much evolved 'Prince.' This Prince seemed more mature and confident with appearances on television and in interviews. It seemed he was more willing to put himself out there as a role model for kids. He also seemed to be more careful about what his image represented. He had come full circle in his life.

Prince had grown from a boy, to a real man on a mission. His mission was to be closer to God and he seemed to achieving that. I believe later in his life he struggled with his desire for sex and his own belief system around the explicit sexual performances he used to love doing. He wanted to be remembered more for doing good than being sexy.

However, I think it will be hard to forget how raw and sexual Prince could be onstage.

As he grew and matured, it was as if his 'female' and 'male' sides merged, to complete his soul as a whole. He looked different to me in his later years on television. He had an aura about him that said he had truly found God.

I always felt Prince and I connected spiritually and didn't need to speak in later years, because we had talked so much on the phone during our romance! I feel there is a beautiful connection between us that will always remain. Prince has been a constant thread in my life, one that will be forever connected to my heart. When people are young, we are still trying to find ourselves and discover who we really are and who we really want to be. Prince and I were at that phase in life when we met thirty years ago. He was battling good and evil, the dark and the light, his ego and alter ego. I think our souls were drawn to each other so that we could learn from each other and discover our true selves.

Friends ask me if Ronn gets jealous of my relationship with Prince and it makes me laugh. Ronn is wise and secure enough as a human being, to know that my relationship with Prince helped make me the woman I am today by his side. There is no need for jealousy and I only wish Prince had lived to meet my amazing husband.

To me, the saddest part of Prince's story is that he died without having a loving relationship towards the end of his life. He died without experiencing the joy of fatherhood. There is no doubt by the time his *Emancipation* CD arrived in the mid '90s, Prince had found true love and happiness with his bride, Mayte. However, the tragedy of losing their child would be something that would eventually tear them apart. And he never got as close to another woman.

I think the simple things in life are what's most important and I feel blessed to have now found the love and the family I wanted so badly throughout my life. I have been with Ronn for twelve years and happily married for seven. I helped him raise two beautiful daughters, who are now twenty-two and seventeen years old.

I think all human beings want to be loved and to give love. Sharing your life with another is what is most important in my opinion. As driven and successful as Prince was, love and family was not something that was top priority for him until late in life. Ultimately this eluded him. Perhaps that's why he focused more on humanitarian work and religion in his later years.

I've always put love first even though I was successful in my career. It felt like the right thing to do and from what I've seen in Hollywood, most people do not do that. At the end of the day, what does all the fame, money and success really mean without true love? I know my career probably would have gone further had I not made some of the decisions for love that I made earlier in my life. Looking back, I wouldn't change a thing. All my decisions made me become the person I am today.

Soon after Prince's death I had a dream about him. It's weird because I seldom remember my dreams unless they are premonition dreams. I have had three premonition dreams in my life and they have all come true! I pay attention to them. In premonition dreams I have trouble waking up and it takes me a moment to differentiate if it was indeed reality, or a dream. I had one such dream before discovering Seth was cheating:

I was alone in Greece on a spiritual cruise to the most Holy places like the house of the Virgin Mary and locations where some of the Bible was written. I was walking down a hotel hallway with Seth when a girl stepped out of a room saying "Hello" to Seth in a very seductive tone. I asked him who she was and he said he didn't know. We continued to walk down the hotel hallway and another girl stepped out of a room and said, "Hello, do you remember Heather?" I again asked who were those girls and he claimed he didn't know. When I arrived back in Los Angeles from Greece, I asked Seth if he knew anyone named Heather.

A couple of weeks later, I discovered Seth had been unfaithful throughout our entire relationship.

Since I've had only three premonition dreams in my life, I can recall the details and they usually are signs that something huge is about to happen in my life. There has always been some truth to them. However, most of time I cannot recall my dreams. But I do recall the dream I had about Prince shortly after his death.

In the dream, Prince was the subject of a photoshoot Ronn and I were producing. Yes, Prince was working for me! He was very calm and even brought his own wardrobe to wear for the shoot. I was just about to say to him, "So can I get that photo I never got with you?" But the photographer called him to set and I didn't let the words out of my mouth.

On waking and contemplating this dream, I found it so profound because I never did press him to take any photos with me and I never worked for him - as much as we both wanted to over the years, timing and circumstances just didn't allow it.

I was never on his payroll. I never tried to further my career by knowing him.

I just loved him. And for a time, he loved me.

Since Prince's death, I often think back to a happier, more innocent time for both of us - the time we spent together in Minneapolis long ago, when he played "Sometimes It Snows In April" for me.

The words touched me deeply then and even more so now...

"Sometimes I wish that life was never ending,
but all good things, they say, never last,
and love, it isn't love, until it's past."

Afterword

My dream about Prince I took to be a sign - that I must pay attention to my intuition and all signs from the universe, more than ever now in the aftermath of his death. I truly believe that my intuition has guided me throughout my life. I've always strived to be the best person I can be, in how I treat myself and in how I treat others. My gut feeling has steered me to know what is right and what is wrong.

It is my intuition that has guided me to write this memoir. In the past weeks, the words have poured out of me. I knew I had to commit it to paper because I didn't want to forget a single detail of the beautiful, magical journey I had with Prince.

I feel he wants me to tell our story now too.

Half of the profit proceeds from this memoir will be donated to:

#YesWeCode.

For more information visit:

www.yeswecode.org

PRINCE DAY

JUNE 7TH

Prince's 58th birthday was June 7th, 2016

After his death, Minneapolis - the city that Prince loved and
called home - officially declared June 7th as 'Prince Day.'

In the years to come, fans from all over the world are invited to
Minneapolis on this day, to celebrate his life and legacy.

Other Titles by Devin Devasquez

The Naked Truth about A Pinup Model

True Age, Timeless Beauty

and with Ronn Moss:
My Husband's A Dog ... My Wife's A Bitch (A Humorous Look at
Relationships.)

www.devindevasquez.com
contact: devin@DevinD.me

20905983R00149

Printed in Great Britain
by Amazon